MAHALIA JACKSON

Darlene Donloe

MS

MELROSE SQUARE PUBLISHING COMPANY
LOS ANGELES, CALIFORNIA

PICTURE CREDITS

DARLENE DUNLOE is a member of the National Association of Black Journalists. Her work has appeared in *People Magazine, Billboard, Essence, Egony, The Hollywood Reporter, Players* and *Black Entertainment Magazine*.

Consulting Editor for Melrose Square
Raymond Friday Locke

Originally published by Holloway House, Los Angeles.
© 1992 by Darlene Donloe.

MAHALIA JACKSON

MELROSE SQUARE BLACK AMERICAN SERIES

CONTENTS

Chapter One

Carnegie Hall

NO ONE COULD HAVE anticipated the tremendous excitement outside of Carnegie Hall. It was still hours before Mahalia Jackson would make her debut and already thousands of fans, mostly black, had gathered on the streets surrounding the concert hall.

New York traffic was jammed even more than usual, and people were packed in tight around the building, all anxious to hear the woman who had been proclaimed the "world's greatest gospel singer".

Inside the hall, Mahalia Jackson was nervous. Very nervous. More nervous then she

---

Mahalia Jackson, "Queen of Gospel Song" at the height of her career. She realized her dream by playing Carnegie Hall on October 1, 1950, followed by a concert tour of Europe.

had ever been in her career. She was not only going to have to prove she deserved her title, but she was playing Carnegie Hall, a place that, before that evening, she had only dreamed of headlining.

After all, this was the "magic circle", the place where classy singers the likes of Caruso, Lily Pons, Paul Robeson, Duke Ellington and Marian Anderson performed. And here she was about to join that illustrious group— Mahalia, the girl from New Orleans, who was once told during a singing lesson to "stop screaming" when she sang so that white people could understand her. That turned out to be her first and last singing lesson.

This was the same woman whose first husband had told her to give up the notion of becoming famous by singing gospel to the masses. The woman who had many obstacles thrown in her path, but always managed to hurdle each one. She had overcome so much and turned so many difficulties into points of growth.

And here she was doing it once again— Mahalia Jackson, the first person ever to give an all-gospel concert in the celebrated hall. This would be a historic event.

But what was she doing here? What in the world could she sing that would hold the at-

Mahalia Jackson singing a gospel song on radio station WHOM. She began her career by singing in churches, then moved on to gospel radio where she soon became a star.

tention of an audience that was 20 percent white? Would they understand what she was trying to say through her performance, or would they sit and look at her in wonderment of how she came to be so powerful in the world of gospel? Was this God's trial? Was she ready for this big step? A lot of questions danced through her head as she paced back and forth in her dressing room. Her hands clasped tight in the prayer position, a chill fell over Mahalia's body. A cold sweat drenched her dress.

Ready or not, it was time for her to go on stage. The Gaye Singers had just finished and now the crowd was tired of waiting.

There was an estimated 8,000 people who had waited in line for hours. Many talked amongst themselves about the woman they had come to hear, pay homage to and revere. They wondered what the woman with the booming voice, spiritual message and power-ful presence would sing? What she would look like? But most of all, how she would sound?

When people came to hear Mahalia Jackson sing, it was as if for one brief moment humani-ty was at peace with itself. She had that calm-ing affect on people. Very few people had touched and transformed the existence of so many others.

Mahalia Jackson was not just a gospel

singer; she was a new kind of gospel singer, one who would come to redefine the art form. She was a woman unlike other women: a breaker of precedence.

The events leading to this moment had left Mahalia a little dizzy. Virtually overnight, she had gone from singing in small churches, to larger black churches, standard concert fields, and now Carnegie Hall. Before she knew it, word had spread around the world about her enormous talent. She began to get offers from everywhere. It seemed everyone wanted Mahalia to come and share her music ministry.

Even so, when she received the invitation to come to New York and sing in the legendary Carnegie Hall, Mahalia was stunned and overwhelmed.

And now here it was, the big night. Mahalia had made it from the streets of New Orleans, to one of the world's most renowned stages.

As she sat in her dressing room preparing to take center stage, she remembered the time she highly protested the possibility that she would even get such a shot. The time when Joe Bostic, a press agent, sports announcer and disc jockey, approached her about producing the concert at Carnegie Hall. At that time she brushed him, and his notions, aside. Mahalia didn't think the kinds of songs she sang were

Mahalia was again invited to sing at the 1958 Democratic National Convention (repeating her 1952 Convention performance).

Adlai E. Stevenson was nominated as the Democratic candidate to run against Dwight D. Eisenhower. She supported Stevenson.

the kinds of songs fit for the reputation of Carnegie. "Carnegie is for the great opera singers. That's for people with class."

Now, years later, someone had forgotten to inform Mahalia of her popularity, her incredible drawing power and her own brand of class.

Still, Mahalia thought her humbleness might be an embarrassment and was convinced that no one wanted to hear gospel at the famous hall. Luckily for everyone, Bostic wore Mahalia down with his persistence. Mahalia would later reveal that she relented only to get rid of Bostic. In fact, Mahalia would later change her mind and write a letter of refusal, thanking Bostic for his interests, but opting to pass on the opportunity. But Bostic was sincere and determined to bring the gospel to Carnegie.

He did.

The performance was sold out and the hall's management was so overwhelmed with people wanting to see the riveting performer that they were forced to place some of the audience on the stage, only inches away from Mahalia.

All day Mahalia had thought of nothing else except performing at her best for "her people". She wanted desperately to get her message across.

Mahalia once said that "man today is crying the blues, whether he sings them or speaks

An unwavering Christian all of her life, Jackson was frequently posed by her recording company, Columbia, so that an attractive church was positioned behind her as in this photograph.

them—neglecting to think of, to use, the divine power within". She wanted to help people find their own power within. "Give God the Glory," she would say. "I don't sing to entertain, but to spread the word." She was always conscious and careful not to have anyone mistake her intentions. God came first and whatever accolades she received were secondary to the task at hand.

The crowd had come from near and far to see and hear Mahalia. Some had traveled from Harlem, others from Boston and Philadelphia to witness Mahalia's triumphant Carnegie appearance.

They were not to be disappointed. Mahalia's nervousness soon took a backseat after she reached the stage and stared out into the faces of the thousands who were pulling for her to have a successful debut.

Mahalia sang, and sang some more.

She started off with "A City Called Heaven" and then "I Walked Into The Garden." No, "I Walked Into The Garden" was not a gospel song, it was more of a ballad.

For a brief moment, Mahalia felt as if she was forcing herself too much. "Calm down," she thought, "be yourself."

Finally, she broke into "Amazing Grace." The result was amazing in itself. The audience began to pace the floor and scream and shout.

When she began to sing, the audience sat spellbound except for the rhythmic clap that followed the gospel beat.

Carnegie was filled with such emotion that it wasn't long before the audience was rejoicing and dancing in the aisles. They had expected a blessing and had received one. Some tapped their feet, others shouted the victory, many cried, while others raised their hands toward heaven proclaiming their love for the Lord and Mahalia.

Everyone, including Mahalia had gotten carried away. With no particular form or fashion, Mahalia came and conquered.

"Oh, sister Jackson," someone screamed. "You are truly a living legend. You lead us, truly, you lead us. "

She had spread the gospel to the delight of everyone in the concert hall. Even more important, Mahalia had redefined gospel music.

It was clear she was a success!

On October 1, 1950, Mahalia Jackson had not only accomplished one of her goals, she received outstanding reviews and had broken all attendance records set by jazzman Benny Goodman and Arturo Toscanini.

The newspapers praised her performance. Well, except the *New York Times,* which simply talked about the distance some people had traveled to see the concert.

As far as a review on Mahalia, the *Times* simply wrote, "the featured singer was Mahalia Jackson."

The *Herald Tribune* wrote that Mahalia "displayed a voice of range and timbre well suited to the character of her music."

But what Mahalia really wanted to know, was what the *New York Amsterdam News* had thought of her performance.

They wrote, "Mahalia Jackson, the diva of all gospel singers. Even more electrifying than her fame. "

Mahalia smiled.

Mahalia always felt that she had to prove something by maintaining her heritage of black songs. She always stressed how important it was to be yourself. "I've never been ashamed of my songs," she said. "I've sung them everywhere even though many of my people didn't want me to. Many of them criticized me for being in high places singing these songs."

Carnegie soon became a friendly and frequent stop.

With that hurdle won, Mahalia set her sights even higher. Up next, a concert tour of Europe.

1923, by Edward Elcha, courtesy of Rudi Blesh.

Blues singer Bessie Smith in 1923. Her first record sold 780,000 copies but earned her only $125. Jackson liked the blues but her father did not allow it to be heard at home.

Chapter Two

Roots

MAHALIA JACKSON WAS BORN on Water Street in New Orleans, Louisiana on October 26, 1911. She was the third daughter in a family of six children, some of whom were her step-siblings. Mahalia was the second child born to her mother, Charity, and her father, John Jackson Jr.

Although her family never had much money and lived in what could only be described as a shack, they made ends meet the best way they could. Mahalia's mother worked as a domestic and her father moved cotton on the river docks during the day and worked as a

In this pen and ink drawing of Bessie Smith by Christopher De Gasperi is the "show biz" Bessie Smith that Mahalia Jackson so admired. Later, she would be compared to Bessie.

barber at night, which left time for him to preach on Sundays.

Mahalia never got a chance to spend a lot of time with her father, though. Before she was born, Mahalia's parents, who were never legally married, would separate and her father, who moved around the corner, would start another family and move them to Upper Carrollton near the Mississippi River.

During that time the practice of living together in that region was not considered unusual. And it was quite all right with City Hall if children from these kinds of relationships took the name of their father. It was more or less an open arrangement, which essentially meant: leave the Negroes to handle their own affairs.

After John Jackson Jr. started his second family, he spent no more time with Mahalia's mother, and not enough time with Mahalia. But Mahalia's love for her father never waned. She loved him very much. Every so often she would go to his barbershop in the evening and sit on his lap and he would call her his little "chocolate drop". Since she couldn't spend a lot of time with him Mahalia's regular routine would be to visit her father's parents who lived nearby, and ask as many questions about him as she could. Mahalia came from a large family. Her mother, Charity, was one of seven Clark sisters, which included, Bell, Duke, Hannah, Alice, Rhoda and Bessie.

Mahalia's family lived on Water Street in what was called the 16th Ward. This section was called the Front of the Town, which means it was right along the levee of a big bend of the Mississippi River.

Mahalia's neighborhood consisted of blacks, Creoles, Italians and French. Everyone got along with everyone else. Many of her friends were white, but it made no difference. They lived next door to each other—and it was no big deal—then. She had plenty of friends and energy to match. Every day the children would go to church and play there as well. Her propensity to sing would come at an early age. She had such a big voice, that even as a toddler they allowed her to sing in the Sunday School choir.

In New Orleans ragtime music and jazz was everywhere. That part of the South was filled with music, from the local cabarets and cafes where entertainers like Jelly Roll Morton and King Oliver performed—to the beautiful showboats that cruised up and down the Mississippi.

Mahalia would hear the blues everywhere she went. After all, she was born and raised in the "first city" of black music. She was deeply moved by the sacred music of the city. From the banks of the river, to walking up and down her own street, Mahalia's world was filled with music.

She was acquainted with the records of Bessie Smith and other blues singers but, when she was at home, her preacher father confined the family's listening habits to strictly religious music. Mahalia would come by her love of music legitimately. Some of her father's cousins were in showbiz. Jeanette Jackson and her husband, Josie Burnette, travelled with singer Ma Rainey, who was called the "Mama of the Blues". Ma Rainey had a "Butterbeans and Susie" comedy act with her tent show in which Mahalia's relatives performed. Mahalia's talents were seen by the troupe, who wanted her to travel with them. However, Mahalia was not allowed to go. Later Mahalia, who was called "Halie" because she was the pet of the family, would say that decision, "changed her whole life".

Still, in her home, everything shut down from Friday night until Monday. She lived in a community and belonged to a church that made sure Christians remained Christians. Missionaries of the church kept a close eye on whether you were attending church and prayer meetings and leading a Christian life. Even if she wanted to, she couldn't get out of hand. Her every move was watched. It didn't bother Mahalia though, because she insisted her strength was in the church.

Mahalia was five when her mother died. It was a terrible blow to a little girl who loved her mother very much. Even more pressing was the issue of who was going to take care of her and her brother, William, who was 10 at the time. Her father was away most of the time and wouldn't be able to care for the children.

Her aunt, Mahalia Paul, for whom she was named, decided to raise Mahalia and her brother. Aunt Duke as she was known throughout the family would prove to be a stiff disciplinarian. She showed little, if any, affection and believed in church and hard work. Although she wasn't the eldest, Bell was, Aunt Duke was the boss whenever she was around. Living with Aunt Duke left little in the form of extras. Halie was allowed one dress and spent most of the time barefoot.

Whenever he could, Halie's father would give her money to take to Aunt Duke to show his appreciation for her providing a home for his children.

Mahalia and the other children looked for-

An early photograph of the waterfront Old Market before it was torn down. Mahalia was born on nearby—and similar— Water Street in what ''can only be described as a shack.''

ward to the weekends. On Saturdays and Sundays they would bathe in big tin tubs in the kitchen. The water was either heated on the stove or outside in the sun. After their legs were rubbed with vaseline, they were ready for anything.

Although she didn't live a fairytale existence, Mahalia had fond memories of growing up in New Orleans. Even after she became a celebrity, the thought of home would move her to tears.

When you live in New Orleans the Mississippi River becomes a part of you. As most children did during that time, Mahalia had to get creative in order to have fun. As a child she never really had a toy or a store-bought doll. She did, however, make her own rag dolls. She would even braid up grass to use for hair.

By some's standards Mahalia's childhood would seem unhappy. She never saw a Christmas tree except in church.

At an early age she was expected to toe the line. Living in Aunt Duke's home there were strict rules to adhere to. Mahalia would have to rise early and scrub floors. She slept on a mattress made of corn shucks and Spanish moss. Each year she would gather the moss and corn shucks and tuck them into her mattress covers. Some days she'd pick up driftwood for firewood. She even learned how to cut sugar cane stalks and palm fronds and weave them into cane chairs.

Growing up in farm country Mahalia got to eat all kinds of food, which was cheap. She and her friends and family would catch fish, shrimp and crabs, and gather okra, green beans, tomatoes, peas and corn. The family kept chickens, possum, rabbit, raccoon and goats.

But even after she could afford to eat whatever she wanted, Mahalia never went for the more high class food. Just give her some biscuits, rice, beans, bacon and shrimp gumbo and she'd be happy.

Baby alligator was also a delicacy. Often Mahalia would have it for breakfast. They'd catch the unsuspecting gator as he rested on the riverbank and then creep up behind him and hit him over the head, knocking him out. The tail was then baked like chicken with herbs, onions and garlic. And then there was the head cheese, actually made with the whole head of a hog. Mahalia would stew the head on the back of the stove until the juice turned to a clear jelly. The recipe called for the juice to be poured into a mold and chilled.

Mahalia always looked forward to Christmas dinner. While she couldn't expect to receive

The Mississippi River waterfront in New Orleans. Mahalia Jackson's father was employed here unloading bales of cotton. The family home was nearby, within walking distance.

gifts, she did expect a true feast cooked up by Aunt Duke.

Christmas dinner would often consist of roast goose and pork, vegetables, raccoon stuffed with sweet potatoes, breads, pies and cakes. This was also the one occasion in which wine was served since it wasn't considered a sin, but rather a kind of tradition of being served wine and sweet cakes when you visited your neighbors.

By the time Halie was seven she was already doing odd jobs at the white folks' house where her Aunt Bessie worked. They both got paid two dollars a week to help get the white kids ready for school and do dishes before they went to school themselves. Then in the afternoon they'd return to help out where needed.

All her life Mahalia was a smart and tough cookie. One day when a bunch of Italian boys jumped on her, she beat three of them and then caught the fourth one the next day and whipped him too. Mahalia didn't consider the incident racially motivated, but rather boys being boys.

She never felt any difference around the white family that her aunt Bessie took her around either. In fact they treated her nicely. She received clothes from them and Halie would always remember the good food that would come from "the pan."

The pan was the extra food white families would share with their colored help after they had eaten and the dishes were done. These were not just scraps of food, but rather casseroles and roasts, vegetables and anything the family had eaten for dinner. Mahalia said the pan saved many families, who, if nothing else, counted on being able to eat good food. After all, they were living in a city known for its good food.

New Orleans is known for jazz and for its Mardi Gras celebration. Mahalia used to love to listen to the bands except on Carnival Day when they had the Zulu Parade. It was then that a lot of killing took place. Mahalia considered Carnival Day the devil's day.

She did, however, like All Saints' Day. Thousands of residents would spend the day with loved ones who had passed on. It was a day that many people spent in the cemeteries decorating and tending the graves of their loved ones. Folks would sing songs and have a picnic on the grounds. This was yet another time for Mahalia to display her talents.

Her favorite time to sing, though, was at Mount Moriah Baptist Church where she sang with the rest of the congregation. As long as she was testifying to the glory of the Lord,

Mahalia was happy. She admittedly got a lot of her influence from the Sanctified Church. It was her belief that the blues and jazz and even rock and roll somehow got their beat from the Sanctified Church.

Whenever she would sing and get a spiritual rhythm going, Mahalia would always tell the white folks who couldn't quite clap in time with her music the right way, "Honey, I know you're enjoying yourself but please don't clap along with me."

The church and Aunt Duke were not the only influences in Mahalia's life. There was also her cousin Fred, Aunt Duke's only son. His nickname was "Chafalaye" after the river near where he was born.

Mahalia loved his energy, his spirit and the fact that he was the only one who knew how to get around Duke's scoldings.

Fred was a grown man by the time Halie was 12. She marveled at his style. He was always neatly coiffed, dressed and ready to go. He was a man about town, who bought lots of blues and jazz records, and someone Halie looked up to.

Unbeknownst to Aunt Duke, Mahalia would play the recordings while Duke was at work. She especially loved the recordings of Bessie Smith, who she would later be compared to.

Black field hands on a Louisiana plantation at the time Mahalia was a child. Her grandparents, Paul and Cecile Clark, worked on a rice plantation in Pointe Coupee Parish south of New Orleans.

A New Orleans Mardi Gras parade. For a week before Ash Wednesday such parades have appeared on the streets several

times daily for decades. However, Mahalia was not allowed to attend because her father considered such displays "sinful."

Smith's music haunted Mahalia. She listened intently because at that time the blues was a way for blacks to ease their burdens and strengthen their will to survive.

But music wasn't the only thing in Mahalia's life. Like other children she went to school. She made it as far as the eighth grade at McDounough School Number 24 before having to leave to earn money. She worked as a laundress working as much as ten hours a day.

One night after work she came home to find Aunt Duke crying and pacing the floor. A telegram had arrived with the bad news that Fred (Chafalaye) was dead. The news was devastating for Aunt Duke and for Mahalia who adored her cousin.

Now that Fred was gone, Mahalia began to get the urge to venture outside of New Orleans. Chicago sure seemed inviting. After all, others had gone and made out okay, why couldn't she. More and more Chicago dominated her thoughts. Halie heard stories about how blacks lived better in Chicago. Stories abounded about how they were able to ride busses with white people, drive their own cars, shop in the same stores and actually mix with them. It was hard to believe. Halie didn't know anything else except the ways of New Orleans. The ways of the South had just always

A New Orleans French Quarter street. Mahalia's family lived nearby in a neighborhood that was made up of Blacks, French, Italians, and both white and brown Creoles.

been accepted.

Determination began to swell in Mahalia, so much so, that finally, in 1928 at the age of 16 she went to Chicago. She used the money she had saved from being a nursemaid and laundress. Of course, Aunt Duke objected, but Mahalia didn't budge. It was time she found out what else life had to offer. She was going to Chicago whether she had Aunt Duke's blessing or not.

The Mississippi River, New Orleans. Ferryboats, such as the one shown here, riverboats, and seagoing ships all docked here. At night Mahalia would listen to "their lonely sounding horns."

Chapter Three

Chicago

THE RIDE ON THE big number four express train heading up North was exhilarating. Mahalia sat on the train with her aunt Hannah, who had offered to help her get on her feet. A million thoughts ran through her head. What would Chicago be like? Would she find the happiness and contentment that everyone talked about? One thing she was sure to find was just how cold it could get in Chicago in December.

The hawk was there to greet Halie as she stepped off the train and into a rushing wind that went clear through to her bones. She had

Mahalia became famous as a gospel singer, at least in the Chicago area, from "spreading the word in song" over radio station WLIB.

never experienced anything as cold as this. But it was okay, she was in Chicago and about to start a new life.

Aunt Hannah hailed a cab and off they went to the South Side. Halie couldn't believe that the white cab driver allowed them to ride in the taxi. It would have been unheard of in New Orleans for blacks to ride in a cab driven by a white person. Chicago was surely going to be different.

Since she had worked as a nursemaid, Mahalia decided she would make nursing her profession.

"It seemed to be one of the important jobs that Negroes could have in the South," Mahalia said. One of her aunts was one of the first black nurses in New Orleans, so the idea of becoming a nurse didn't seem farfetched.

Next she would set her sights on studying beauty. Mahalia had big plans. But they would have to be put on hold. Her dreams would have to wait a little longer.

Aunt Hannah had suffered a heart attack. Thoughts of attending school took a back seat. Mahalia had to go back to domestic work. She found work as a hotel maid where she made $7.50 a week and in a date-packing factory where she earned $7.20 a week.

Once again she was back to working for

white families. Although she was unhappy in her present situation, Mahalia was taught work ethics and a strong sense of family. What she did, she did out of love. The work hours were long, but Mahalia persevered. Eventually, she found solace in the Greater Salem Baptist Church, which had an all black congregation. She didn't know then just how big a role that church would have on her singing career.

In 1930, soon after joining the church, she began singing in the choir and touring the city's small churches with a group she helped form called the Johnson Gospel Singers, composed of three brothers—Robert, Prince Wilbur and Louise Lemon.

"I suppose that was actually the beginning of my career," Mahalia said. "After that, everybody asked me to sing."

The group started out performing in plays at church socials. Robert Johnson wrote the scripts, acted and directed. Mahalia also performed in the one-acts, which included, "The Fatal Wedding," "Hell-Bound" and "From Earth to Glory."

The quintet was invited to appear at revivals and churches in the Chicago area. In short order the Johnson Singers, whose primary home was the Greater Salem Baptist Church, became very popular around the city. Mahalia felt the group's success had a lot to do with their bounce. While the group would sing the traditional spirituals, they would put their own signature to each song, which usually made them a bit more uptempo.

Besides singing the praises of the Lord, the group also helped churches stay afloat by raising money through concerts around the city. The Johnson Singers helped save many a church. They had become so popular that churches were able to charge nominal admission fees whenever the group agreed to perform.

On a good night the group would make $1.50 for performing. For one performance at Olivet Baptist Church the group received three dollars. Mahalia, whose paycheck often went right back to the church, thought it was great because these occasions were the first times she had received any money in the church. She was overwhelmed when the group received four dollars for singing at the Pilgrim Baptist Church.

It was enough for Mahalia to pay her share of the food and rent at her aunt Hannah's house.

On one occasion she had as much as $4 saved up. She and a friend went to see a music teacher named Dubois to get some pointers. He had once had a career as a concert and operatic singer. For starters he had Mahalia sing a song called "Standing in the Need of Prayer." When she was finished it was clear Professor Dubois did not appreciate her rendition.

"That's no way to sing that song," he said. "Slow down. Sing it like this."

Mahalia didn't like his way.

"You've got to stop hollering," Dubois said. "The way you sing is not a credit to the Negro race. You've got to learn to sing songs so that white people can understand them."

Mahalia disagreed with his assessment. Her friend, though, had obviously impressed Dubois, who told her she had possibilities. Reluctantly, Mahalia handed Dubois the four dollars and left. She was confused, angry and hurt. She couldn't understand why a black man was telling her to sing for white folks, when she was black.

That was it for singing lessons. She never had another one. It was then Mahalia made it up in her mind to sing her songs her way.

As the invitations began to pour in for the group, the compliments about Mahalia's singing increased as well. So did the criticism from some pastors who disagreed with Mahalia's interpretation of the more traditional music. No one in the North had sang the gospel like

Mahalia. She was unique in her performance and her sound. She found the restrictive conventions of traditional gospel music too confining. The conservative churches branded her a rebellious upstart, but that didn't slow her down.

One pastor, after listening to the Johnson Singers, shocked Mahalia by calling her performance "blasphemous" and asked that the group "get that twisting and that jazz" out of his church.

Mahalia stood her ground and proudly told the pastor "this is the way we sing down South! I been singing this way all my life in church!"

Mahalia spent seven years with the Johnson Singers before going solo in 1941. She didn't feel the other singers cared about singing gospel the way she did, so she left the group.

By listening to other singers intently, Mahalia had developed her own voice with no formal training. She was on her way to achieving an incredible reputation as a gospel singer.

Although she had never made a record, Mahalia was quickly becoming known all over the country as she criss-crossed on her numerous gospel crusades. Like a sore thumb it stuck out that most of her audience was made up of black people. During that time whites and blacks did not worship together.

"White people might come over here to Negro churches, and a white minister might invite a few of my people to worship in his church, but that's about all," she said.

This truly disturbed Mahalia. She was quite vocal about her disdain for segregation among the churches. She felt that blacks and whites should serve God together.

"If not, something is wrong with our churches."

Mahalia was unlike any other singer who had come along. Any gospel singer that is. Of course, the comparisons to Bessie Smith were never ending. But there were no gospel legends for her to look to for inspiration. Mahalia would become the meter by which every other gospel singer would be judged.

Because of her rich contralto, Mahalia was approached by an endless procession of music industry professionals to become a blues singer like her idol, Bessie Smith or Ma Rainey. The thought never crossed her mind.

Though she wasn't a blues singer, and never considered herself one, her story belongs with those of Rainey and Smith because gospel, blues and jazz are interrelated aspects of black American music. You can't consider one without the other.

But Mahalia was a devoted church woman. God came first in her life. She wanted to sing songs of hope and praise, not songs of despair. People would tell her, "Girl, you could be a blues singer." She'd answer, "What Negro couldn't be a blues singer?"

It wasn't long before Mahalia's popularity took flight. In the early 1930s, she began to make more money singing at funerals and churches. Her voice took her from Chicago, to New York, to California. Sometimes all she received was a nickel a night. But that was all right with Mahalia, she was happy because she was singing for the Lord. Besides, she was making more money singing in the churches than she could cleaning the white folks' houses.

During a lull in her travels, Mahalia got a job packing dates for seven dollars a week. The job was monotonous and Mahalia grew impatient. This was not what she wanted. After a short time she left and got a job as a maid in a hotel. Each day she would clean thirty-three rooms. At the end of the week she'd receive $12 for her efforts. The job lasted two years.

Soon thereafter she met a black musician named Professor A. Dorsey, who, at one time, was a piano player for Ma Rainey. They travelled together to some of the same church conventions. Mahalia enjoyed the songs Dorsey wrote like "Peace in the Valley"and "Precious Lord." She liked them because they had a nice beat and great rhythm.

Mahalia wasn't into singing the straight laced European sounding songs. She put blue notes in gospel. She would growl and shout and was also known for dancing to the glory of the Lord, strutting and hiking up her dress whenever she felt like it.

She preferred to sing songs that gave her and her audience a lift and even told one minister that very thing when he spoke out against her style in church one evening.

Mahalia reminded him about Psalm 47 which said: "Oh, clap your hands, all ye people; shout unto God with the voice of triumph." That's what she intended to do. She had nothing against European music, she just preferred what she called "Negro music," which always made her feel warm—like she was receiving a letter from home. It never mattered where she sang, because she took the church with her.

When Mahalia sang she felt close to God. She was convinced that her way of singing was what the Lord wanted her to do. Her closeness to the Heavenly Father grew even deeper after Mahalia was convinced he heard one of her prayers.

In the summer of 1934 her grandfather Paul came up to Chicago from New Orleans for a visit. It was a hot summer, so hot that most people cooled off by drinking lots of lemonade and staying in the shade as much as possible. The family made a big deal out of grandfather Paul's visit and treated him royally.

Mahalia came up with the idea that he should have his picture taken before he left. With Mahalia's persistence he decided to go to the studio with Mahalia's cousin Alice.

A short time later Alice phoned to say that Grandfather Paul had a stroke and collapsed. By the time Mahalia and Aunt Hannah got to the hospital he was barely breathing. The doctors didn't give him much of a chance of surviving. Aunt Hannah blamed Mahalia for sending the old man out in the summer heat. She said if he died it was on Mahalia's shoulders.

Needless to say, Mahalia was devastated. She prayed to the Lord for forgiveness and begged him to let her grandfather live. She promised that if he pulled through she would never again attend a motion picture or vaudeville show. These were some of Mahalia's favorite pastimes.

Mahalia's prayers were answered. After two weeks Grandfather Paul walked out of the hospital and went back home strong and healthy. Mahalia never went to a theater again.

While she enjoyed the theater, the attraction of show business never clouded Mahalia's vision. When she began to become more and more popular and the money started coming in regularly, she never lost sight of her mission in life. Sure, she could buy the material things she wanted. But Mahalia was a simple woman. Just give her a clean house and a nice kitchen where she could cook her favorite foods. Mahalia often said she was happiest when she was cooking for a crowd of people.

Chapter Four

I Like
Ike

IT'S TRUE THAT MAHALIA Jackson was devoted to the church and that God was first in her life. It's also true that this first woman of gospel had feelings and yearnings like any other red-blooded individual. In 1935 while attending a church social, Mahalia met a tall, handsome black man named Isaac (Ike) Hockenhull. A graduate of Fisk University and the Tuskegee Institute who had studied to be a chemist, Hockenhull had become a mailman for the post office. The Depression had left a shortage of jobs for chemists and Hockenhull was forced to make a living the best way he

Mahalia Jackson in a relaxed mood. She moved to Chicago at the age of sixteen, with money she had saved from being a nursemaid. Her Aunt Duke objected but Mahalia was determined.

knew how.

Mahalia, who was twenty-four at the time, liked Ike, who was ten years her senior, very much, although she was a little insecure about the way he might feel about her. After all, he was an educated, classy and attractive man. She wondered what interest he would have in her. She had only finished the eighth grade.

But Ike saw past Mahalia's level of education. He liked her a lot and began courting her by bringing her flowers and candy. Often he would visit her in the evening—spending time with Aunt Hannah and Alice so as not to look too eager.

Ike believed in Mahalia's talents. He encouraged her career and believed she could be a great concert artist. So much so, that he offered to guide Mahalia's career.

Within a year the two were married. They lived with Mahalia's aunt Hannah while Ike worked and Mahalia continued to sing and clean in between performances.

Ike was a diligent, persistent man, who was not about to let the Depression keep him down. He worked at any job he could find until he and Mahalia finally got enough money together to get their own apartment.

Before the Depression hit, Ike's mother had a thriving cosmetics business in St. Louis. Her cosmetics line was called "Madame Walker." The creams and lotions sold very well. Since Ike knew the formulas, he used his training as a chemist to mix up assortments of powders and oils.

Mahalia and Ike often stayed up into the wee hours bottling the solutions. Ike would try to sell them in Chicago, while Mahalia tried to sell them on the road. Actually, she sold quite a bit of the product on the road.

Still, the hard times continued. Mahalia's travels increased and Ike's unhappiness with her itinerary also increased. Ike wasn't convinced that gospel was the way for Mahalia to go. He continued to try to persuade his wife to become a concert singer. But Mahalia would have none of it.

"Why do you want to waste your wonderful voice on that stuff?" he would shout. "It's not art!"

Mahalia tried to convince Ike, who wasn't as into the church as she was, that gospel was her destiny. Singing the gospel is what the Lord wanted her to do. The more she tried to convince him, the more the gap between the two of them began to spread.

It was true that Mahalia probably could have been a very successful concert singer. Both Louis Armstrong and Earl "Fatha" Hines

President Dwight D. Eisenhower and Mahalia Jackson on January 3, 1960. After he became a fan, Eisenhower invited her to the White House on two occasions.

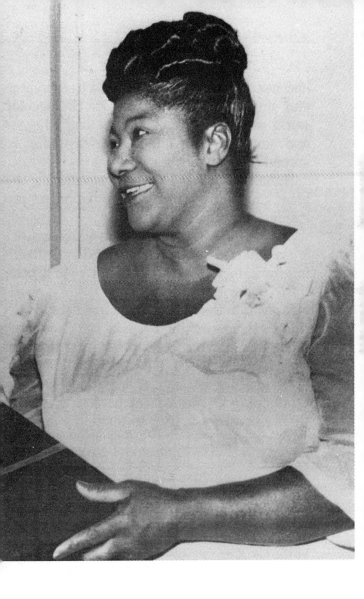

had heard about her and invited her to come and sing with their bands. But the secular world was not for Mahalia. She had a bigger and better plan in mind. She was going to spread God's word her way!

Mahalia often told people that singing the blues could only leave a person feeling empty inside.

"I tell people that the person who sings only the blues is like someone in a deep pit yelling for help, and I'm simply not in that position."

A position that Mahalia did feel herself getting into was starting to make her uncomfortable. She started to get the feeling that she was going to have to choose between her marriage and her mission. It was a decision she was hoping she would not have to make.

Ike's constant urging to make the move to the theater and secular music was beginning to wear thin. He had clipped an ad from the newspaper about a theater project that was casting an all black company of The Mikado.

A leading role in the production was up for grabs. Ike wanted Mahalia to audition for the part. He was certain that she could win the part hands down if she'd only go and sing for them. Mahalia told him the theater was not the place for her. Ike reminded her that they had no money in the house and that it was up to her to do her share. The theater job would pay $60 a week.

Finally, Mahalia gave in. She went to the audition and watched the girls take center stage one by one. Each time one girl got up to audition, Mahalia would fall back in line hoping that by the time they got to her— someone else would have won the part.

No such luck.

Suddenly it was her turn. She sang "Sometimes I Feel Like A Motherless Child." When she was through, you could have heard a pin drop. You also could have heard Mahalia's heart drop. Deep down inside she knew that she had won the audition. She left the theater miserable, hoping that she was wrong and that one of the other girls who had auditioned had somehow impressed the judges even more.

By the time Mahalia got home, Ike had already received the news. Mahalia had won the part and they wanted her to start rehearsals immediately.

Ike was sure this was going to be Mahalia's big break. Mahalia was sure she wanted no parts of the theater. She wondered what the church would think.

Mahalia was not the only one who had gotten a job. Ike had also managed to procure employment selling insurance. Mahalia's prayers were answered. If Ike had a job, she wouldn't have to work.

"You got a job," Mahalia cried. "Then that settles it. I'm not going to any rehearsal. I'm quitting right now."

Needless to say, Ike was livid. He couldn't believe what he was hearing. At that moment he knew that he would not be able to convince her to keep the job.

Their marriage would never be the same. It could not survive the two different lifestyles that its participants were living.

Between Ike's disdain for gospel songs and Mahalia's disregard for Ike's love of the race track, their marriage was dying a slow death. Ike became such a good handicapper that he was nicknamed "Seeing-Eye Ike". Once he even won two thousand dollars and gave it to Mahalia to hold. While Mahalia was gone to Detroit to perform, Ike found the money she had hid for him and spent it all on a race horse.

Soon thereafter the marriage dissolved, though the two remained friends.

Mitch Miller, who worked with Mahalia at Columbia records, with a very young Johnnie Ray. Ray, who "cried" his way to world fame, was a self-proclaimed fan of Mahalia Jackson.

Chapter Five

The Business of The Business

WITH HER MARRIAGE to Ike Huckenhull over, Mahalia was ready to get on with her life. It was now the late 1930s, the Depression was over and Mahalia was looking forward to improving herself.

Her singing had become in such demand that she was finally able to quit working as a maid and concentrate on singing and going to school. With the little bit of money she had managed to save, she attended the Scott Institute of Beauty Culture to learn to be a hairdresser.

In 1939 she opened "Mahalia's Beauty

Mahalia, again at Carnegie Hall. Her fans crossed all color and religious lines. She was nearly as popular in Europe as she was in the United States and had Jewish fans in Israel.

Salon." Luckily for her, she didn't have to advertise. Most of her clients came because they knew her through the church.

Mahalia was determined to make every facet of her life successful. She worked relentlessly at the beauty parlor during the day. On the weekends she would ride the trains to Detroit and St. Louis for singing engagements always making sure she was back in time to open up her shop that next morning.

With the success of the beauty parlor, Mahalia was able to open up a floral shop as well. She was truly becoming a business-woman. The florist business proved to be lucrative. People were always asking her to sing at funerals. Clients bought the flowers as long as Mahalia promised to sing at the funerals. Mahalia happily obliged.

Even with two businesses Mahalia managed to keep her singing career going. Soon she was so well known that music critics began writing about her. She was singing in big gospel tents, ballrooms and small store-front churches.

This was during a time when the jazz bands and nightclub singers were just beginning to debut on the music scene. Some of the greatest blues singers like Muddy Waters, Ivory Joe Hunter and Memphis Slim were selling lots of records in the black world of music.

As the offers to sing poured in, Mahalia realized she was really in business and would quickly have to learn this new world she had entered. She wanted to know every facet of the business. In fact, one night when she climbed into the ticket booth to sell tickets to her own concert, a newspaper reporter joked that if she kept it up a photographer was going to take her picture selling the tickets.

"That's all right, child," Mahalia said. "That'll show some of these dishonest promoters I got sense enough to protect my money."

Mahalia was not going to be a pushover. With as much vigor as she had when she fought the five Italian boys who jumped on her as a kid, Halie was determined not to get cheated out of the money she earned singing the gospel. She had noticed the enormous interest that gospel music was getting from people who didn't really have the church's best interest at heart. She didn't want to become one of the unscrupulous promoter's easy targets. Because of her following Mahalia was getting more than her share of propositions on the road.

The promoters had started to use such zany, outlandish tactics that Mahalia was forced to ask for her money before she ever opened her mouth to sing.

That was never more evident than the time Mahalia was scheduled to sing in a stadium in Philadelphia. When she got there the promoter had switched Mahalia's performance to the following day.

In the mean time, he informed her, she could earn more money by singing in a concert in Newark, if she wanted to because he had connections.

When Mahalia arrived at the concert hall in Newark she was beside herself. There in big bold letters up on a billboard was her name. Upset, Mahalia told the promoter she was not going to sing and to take her name off of the marquee. With a crowd pouring into the auditorium the promoter was starting to get nervous. He had promised the crowd Mahalia Jackson. The people began to grow restless.

Backed into a corner the promoter could do nothing but pay Mahalia her money before she walked out on stage. After putting the roll of bills in her purse, Mahalia went out to sing for the people. Afterwards she drove back to Philadelphia.

The next night Mahalia went to sing for the Philadelphia promoter, although she never told him what had happened the night before. He also acted as if everything was fine.

After the concert Mahalia attended a party at the promoter's home. At the party Mahalia asked for her money. The promoter said he had heard that she had gotten paid the night before and was looking for his share of the money.

Mahalia refused to give him any of the money since she had done the actual singing. She wanted her money and she wasn't going to leave his home until she got it.

The promoter was so upset he left the room and returned with a gun. No one was hurt, but Mahalia saw just what kind of people she was dealing with.

The next morning she was surprised when the Philadelphia promoter showed up at her door with the police. He wanted his half of her earnings.

Mahalia had to go to court and convince the police that he was not entitled to any of the money she had received in Newark. The police sided with Mahalia and the incident was over. That, of course, was the last time Mahalia worked with that particular Philadelphia promoter. Having bounced back from that nightmare, Mahalia made it a rule not to work with unprincipled promoters, but rather to sing only for respected civic organizations.

Chapter Six

On The Move

SINCE THE FIRST DAY she began singing in large concert halls, people wanted Mahalia to act grand and forget about the past.

"Some people act so grand, you can't hand them a letter from home," she said.

But not Mahalia. She had lived with little or nothing as a child. Success to her just meant that more people were listening to the words of the Lord. It was a message that Mahalia had received a long time ago.

She believed that spiritual singers were angels of peace spreading songs of quality and

Mahalia Jackson, the all time top selling gospel singer, in a publicity photograph shot in 1954, the year her radio program made its debut on the CBS radio network.

good will. She, herself, had become an ambassador of love.

To her, the audience was part of her family.

"When I walk on stage, I forget I'm a singer," she said. "My singing is not to entertain. I feel something, the weight of the world."

In her own small way Mahalia wanted to bring a message of hope to people—whether it was through her music, or by personal contact.

Even during the Depression when times were hard for everyone, Mahalia tried to bring comfort to others. When she sang people would give her pennies and nickels. She would take whatever money she received and buy coal for churches.

One day after she had earned $1.75 washing clothes, Mahalia passed a bunch of people in a soup line. She invited them all to her house where she fixed up a mess of potatoes, beans, hamhocks, neckbones and rice. She fed twenty people. It then became a habit for her whenever she got money, to go to the 2nd Ward and bring people home and feed them food that would stick to their ribs. Mahalia just couldn't walk by people living on the streets.

A reporter once asked Halie how she compared her dedication to the Lord as opposed to a regular Sunday churchgoer.

"Do you know the story about the chicken and the pig," she asked. He hadn't heard. "Well you see there was a chicken and a pig strolling down Main street together. They crossed against a red light, past a restaurant known for it's bacon and eggs. You know, the chicken boasted, 'if it weren't for my eggs this place wouldn't be famous.' 'That might be true, said Mr. Pig. 'But for you it's a commitment, for me, it's a total sacrifice.'"

That story summed up how Mahalia lived her life. She didn't half-step when it came to serving the Lord.

In a strange way the Depression was one of the reasons why Mahalia began her gospel singing career. The other, of course, was her love for the church.

About the same time she left the Johnson Gospel Singers, gospel music was beginning to spread its wings and take flight. Blacks could relate to the music because it often spoke to the times and the era in which they lived.

The genre incorporated elements from history, religion and literature. Performance also played an important and pivotal role because improvisation has always been important to the African tradition.

Many believe it is the performance that gives the song its definition and determines its melody, cadence and rhythm, as well as the perception of the listener.

Black spirituals, which are filled with psychological symbols of estrangement, autocracy and a desire to escape slavery, don't really concern themselves with sin, but rather the troubles of the world.

The origin of spirituals dates back to the black race. Some have said that spirituals represented the expression of anguish experienced by human beings in bondage, particularly black slaves. The question of the origins of gospel music included not only the influence of British music upon African music but also the effects of the combination of a number of varied West African musics.

The spirituals of black southerners and white southerners is different. Blacks gathered their materials from a variety of sources and shaped them into their own distinctive artistic property. Controversy has followed the origins of the genre. Some have said spirituals, which have the tendency to harmonize in thirds (also used widely in West Africa) had been composed partly under the influence of association with whites and partly actually imitated from their music.

Some scholars have mutually agreed that one characteristic of the black spritiual is the beat, and pulsating rhythm that flows through black music. The same, they say, cannot be felt to the same degree in white music.

James Weldon Johnson wrote: The Negro loves nothing better in his music than to play with the fundamental time beat. He will, as it were, take this fundamental throb and pound it out with his left hand almost monotonously; while with his right hand he will take as many liberties with it as he dares to take without losing the beat.

Johnson added that "the Negro took as his basic materials his native African rhythms and the King James Version of the Bible and out of them created the spirituals."

Spirituals and the blues are very close in their characteristics. That may be one of the reasons why Mahalia felt such a bond with blues singer Bessie Smith. The blues first surfaced in minstrel shows in the South in the late 1800s. The Rabbit Foot Minstrels featured a singer who would come to be known as Ma Rainey because she fostered the classic blues style. Not surprisingly, Rainey was the force behind Bessie Smith, who was her protege. Rainey was the "Mother of the Blues", Smith, the "Empress of the Blues" and Mahalia, the

"World's Greatest Gospel Singer."

Before Mahalia left the Johnson Singers, one of the group's performances was heard by Thomas A. Dorsey, a pianist, composer and arranger who had done a lot of work for singer Ma Rainey. Mahalia had met him in 1929 at the Pilgrim Baptist Church. Dorsey eventually persuaded Mahalia to sing some of his songs. She also sold his songs on street corners in the early 1930s and at various storefront churches.

During the 1930s Mahalia's popularity had grown tremendously. In 1937, she was invited to record for Decca Records. Her first outing was not a big success. In fact, the music got little, if any, attention. It would be almost a decade later before Mahalia would venture into the recording studio again.

But she did.

In 1945 her national fame rose with "Move On Up a Little Higher," which sold more than one million copies. This was the first time gospel music had been brought to the general public. Europeans critics were also beginning to pay attention. The song would eventually sell eight million copies on the Apollo label.

The next year her partnership with Dorsey ended. The partnership had lasted since 1940 when he had become her official accompanist.

Dorsey, whose nickname was "Georgia Tom," was a composer and pianist for tent shows. He worked, primarily, with Gertrude "Ma" Rainey.

He also started one of the first gospel mail order businesses in the country. He started by getting a job transcribing on paper the singers' blues J. Mayo "Ink" Williams cut for Paramount Records. No white arrangers were doing it at the time.

There wasn't a market for what was called "race records." Dorsey desperately wanted to get into spirituals, but there wasn't a lot of interest at the time.

If the black market bought anything it was the blues, not spirituals. Feeling frustrated, Dorsey acquired a list of church addresses, borrowed money to print the song, "Some Day, Somewhere". He sent out thousands of inquiries, and there began his mail order business.

Mahalia would actually stand on street corners and sing the songs. Usually whoever heard her would be so impressed, they'd spend the dime to get a music sheet of the song. Sometimes they would sell five thousand copies a day.

There weren't a whole lot of gospel singers around during this time. The only other with any kind of a following was Sallie Martin.

Mahalia was bold during these times. She did what many considered "going out on a limb" by singing in such an uptempo way. But Mahalia didn't care. She didn't care that some people looked down their noses at her. She didn't care that some preachers would not receive her and others would cut her down from their pulpits.

Some who heard her during her cross country crusades admired her conviction and artistry. More and more people began to tell her to become a blues singer. But Mahalia knew that wasn't the life for her.

She was even offered as much as $25,000 to perform in Las Vegas clubs. She turned them down. "I'd rather sing about 'old man Jesus' than about some old man some woman has lost." Mahalia was certain she was doing what she was called to do. If they didn't like her style, then all it meant was that it was not for them. But it was for somebody.

In 1948 she became the co-founder (with Theodore Frye) of the National Baptist Music Convention, an auxiliary to the National Baptist Convention. By that time she had become well known throughout the church circuit.

Mahalia perhaps was responsible more than any other single person for bringing gospel to the attention of the world, she would go on to establish many milestones in its history.

By 1950 she gave the first all-gospel concert at Carnegie Hall, and she started making appearances on television. All of this was done under the management of Joe Bostic.

In 1952 she was awarded the French Academy of Music prize for her record, "I Put My Trust in Jesus." She wanted to thank the French people personally, so she went to Paris to sing. Thus began her first European tour. The audience loved her and greeted her with great enthusiasm. They had never heard anyone like Mahalia before. But to see her in person was even more powerful. She received twenty-one curtain calls.

MOVE ON UP A LITTLE HIGHER

WORDS AND MUSIC

by

Rev. W. HERBERT BREWSTER

A BOWLES ARRANGEMENT

ARRANGED

by

W. O. HOYLE

Price 15 Cents

PUBLISHED BY

BOWLES MUSIC HOUSE

4640 S. STATE STREET   CHICAGO, ILL.

Chapter Seven

The European Tour

W ITH HER LARGE FOLLOWING and booming, distinct voice, it was inevitable that Mahalia would venture into the recording industry.

She believed that gospel was great American music. And, although she wasn't sure if she acccepted "pop gospel", or "soul music," she was convinced that both genres would be mainstays within the industry. She was also sure that both types of music would make their way into the white mainstream just like all the other forms of traditional black music had, like the blues and jazz.

In 1947 Mahalia Jackson recorded the Rev. Herbert Brewster's "Move On Up A Little Higher" and made it a huge hit. The record sold over 2 million copies.

In 1934 she recorded her first record for Decca Records. The song was "God Gonna Separate the Wheat From the Tares." It didn't sell a million copies, but it did okay by gospel song standards.

While in the recording studio practicing Mahalia began to sing a song she had known since she was a child. Unbeknownst to her, Ink Williams from Decca Records was in the studio listening to her. He liked what he heard and asked her to record the song for the label. She did, and in 1946 Halie achieved widespread acclaim with her recording of "I Will Move On Up A Little Higher," which became a top record on the Apollo records label.

Halie had become a celebrity among black fans who were gobbling up the record as fast as the record company could press them. Almost two million copies were sold.

Her voice had become an inspiration for many. Her keen sense of timing, phrasing and eloquence had become her signature. She was, as many had proclaimed, the "Queen of Gospel Song."

The queen's royal subjects were getting more and more impatient. They just couldn't seem to get enough of Mahalia. She started getting requests to sing from across the country, including the National Baptist Convention, and even the "Ed Sullivan Show."

But the requests that would throw her for a loop was the invitation that came to sing at Carnegie Hall. After her first concert in 1950, Mahalia was a regular at the famous venue. With Carnegie Hall clearly in her back pocket, it was time for Mahalia to conquer other concert halls.

Europe seemed the most likely challenge to go after. After all, everyone was telling her to consider a European tour and people in France and Denmark had actually written asking her to come and sing for them. It shouldn't have been a complete surprise to Mahalia that her popularity had managed to cross the water. After all, she was considered the chief reason for the popularization of gospel songs during the 50s.

After winning an award in 1952 from the French Academy of Music for her record, "I Can Put My Trust in Jesus," Mahalia decided to travel to Europe.

If the people of France were "nice enough" to give her a prize, she ought to be enough of a lady to go and say "Thank you." Admittedly, she was a little worried about whether or not Europeans would understand what it was she was saying with her music.

She was pleasantly surprised. While the

English were too staunch to let their hair down, the French and the Danish really got into the gospel.

The Europeans proved to be religious people, saints, sinners and rock n' rollers. The way they carried on, one would think there was a revival meeting going on.

The people in Sweden had waited in the pouring rain for hours to see and hear Mahalia. In Berlin, where she sang "We Shall Overcome," she overwhelmed them. People packed the hall to hear the gospel. That was also the place where she got one of her biggest chills. Someone told her the last time he heard people chant like they had for her—was for Hitler in 1938. Still, she felt proud, but she didn't want to kid herself.

Sure she loved singing in Europe. The people were emotional and enthusiastic. They thought of her as a great singer. They followed her around and treated her real grand.

"For a moment or two there's a bit of vanity and the feeling of success. But when God gets a hold of me, I take inventory of myself. I know it wasn't me."

A magazine writer once said to her, "I never believed in God, but when you sing, I get goose bumps." Mahalia replied, "Those ain't good bumps. That's your soul speaking and you don't even know it's there."

Backstage before each program Mahalia would read from her Bible. That way when she began to sing on stage her strong faith would shine through. She trusted in the Creator.

When the concerts were finished she'd go backstage, wipe the sweat from her brow, the hair from her face and sit down to drink and eat a little. When she knew she had given her all, her usual response was, "I have truly worked for the Lord tonight."

Before the tour was through, Mahalia would visit France, Holland, Belgium, Denmark and London. Not only were her concerts a success, but the European fans even ordered fifty thousand copies of her song, "Silent Night."

Some people considered Mahalia a bit naive. She believed in humanity, faith and hope and wanted people to get to know each other.

"You can't give up hope of us all being one brotherhood." She truly believed in the song, "Let There Be Peace On Earth."

Mahalia couldn't believe how well the Europeans took to her. They filled the concert halls in Cambridge and London. The morning before her exclusive British appearance, Mahalia walked around the city, prayed and ate liver and spinach to get her strength up. This was the big moment. She was to perform at the Royal Albert Hall. The London audience greeted her with great enthusiasm. Unfortunately Mahalia was so sick she was barely able to move. This would be the first time she hadn't touched the people the way she really wanted to. She felt as if the big hall had defeated her.

In Sweden a priest said it was the first time his church had been filled to capacity. In Paris, where she received 21 curtain calls, the crowds were so big the police were called in to maintain control.

People flocked to see Mahalia just like they had flocked to see the secular performers. Perhaps they were attracted to her because of the simplicity of her ways. She was "just a good strong Louisiana woman who can cook rice so every grain stands by itself." It didn't matter that in some of the countries they couldn't understand a word Mahalia was singing. The spirit of the Lord was moving, you didn't need words to interpret that.

Life got lonely far from Chicago. The stage was sometimes very cold. Although she loved giving God the glory there were times after a concert that she would go back to her room and think about home. There was no place like home. But Mahalia knew she had to look beyond her personal needs.

The Golden Gate Quintet. The road Jackson had a huge role in pioneering, gospel music recording, made it possible for many such gospel groups to reach the public in the 1940s.

Mahalia's desires to sing the praises of the Lord around the world were lofty. Her head was ready, but her body began to wear down from all the travelling and singing she had done over the years. She lost 90 pounds in three months and was often too weak to stand. Through the turmoil and the excitement, she was taken with a new wave of nervous exhaustion. Her steps got shorter and her walk was taking a little longer. The one night stands had taken their toll. Off stage she was a tired and sick lady. But on stage she was a ball of fire.

Mahalia was a trooper. No one could stop her from singing. She continued to sing ignoring the signs her body was giving her. As long as the crowd loved her she was willing to change outfits and go on singing for hours.

"I love singing gospel songs," she said. "Very few people are doing what they love. I do well. I get three meals a day, clothes and a house. I'm doing as good as any pop singer. You can only wear one dress at a time."

To gain strength for her concerts, Mahalia would rest all day until it was time to hit the stage. Finally, her body could take no more. She fainted on stage in France. The European tour was cut short.

Doctors in Europe advised Mahalia to have the operation she needed in Paris because being moved back to Chicago could kill her.

Mahalia didn't care. She wanted to go home. She sent a cable to Chicago asking for an ambulance to meet them at the airport in New York. Everyone was worried about the trip but Mahalia.

Surprisingly to everyone, she was very calm even though the weather was bad and she was feeling even worse.

Mahalia took hold of her Bible and boarded the plane. She sang softly to herself the words to "You'll Never Walk Alone."

By the time Mahalia had reached New York, which was two hours past schedule, the ambulance had left and Mahalia's condition had worsened. She decided to go to a friend's house to rest until she could be checked into a hospital in the morning.

She went over to her Aunt Hannah's and asked Mildred to make sure no one knew she was there. On November 26, Mahalia went into the hospital. Just before she went under the anesthetic she asked for the 27th Psalm to be read...Now she was ready.

Mahalia had a hysterectomy. When it was all over, she felt fine. In fact doctors were surprised that she was in such good spirits.

Even though Mahalia had already made a name for herself around the world, some of the doctors who treated her had no idea who she was. However, Dr. Billings' staff, which was mostly black, did know who she was and treated her like family. A number of them even attended the same church as Mahalia.

She received a number of cards, letters and flowers, which made the healing process a lot quicker.

The white press did write about Mahalia's operation, although they didn't give it nearly the same attention as the black press.

The white press wrote : "Mahalia Jackson of 3728 S. Prairie, gospel singer and recording artist, was reported recovering satisfactorily after undergoing surgery"; that a "bronchial ailment" forced cancellation of her European tour." They described her as the "official soloist for the 4 million Negroes of the National Baptist Convention."

The black media blew up the story. Many were worried about Mahalia's health. The reports about her ailment varied. Some believed it was a bronchial ailment as they were told. Some reported she was suffering from nervous exhaustion, while others reported she had her appendix removed.

Mahalia was a very private person and wanted the hysterectomy kept secret.

Thousands of calls came to the hospital trying to wish the singer well. Since many of the calls could not get through, people just began to pray for her.

By the time she checked out of the hospital on December 12, Mahalia felt she had a new body.

The operation was a success and Mahalia threw herself back into her work.

It didn't matter where she was needed. If she was able Mahalia would spread the gospel at the drop of a hat.

On one occasion Mahalia had just returned from the South to find she had a stack of contracts for her to appear in the Carolinas. She was right in the middle of pulling off her clothes when she announced she would return. Mildred couldn't believe it.

"We just came from down that way," said Mildred who was not looking forward to another trip in the black Buick.

Mahalia didn't care. If she was under contract to sing somewhere, she was not going to disappoint the people.

"I'll take the train," Mahalia said. "Cause I got to sing."

She sent her entourage on ahead to let the people know she would be there in time to sing.

Mahalia's train was due in only 10 minutes

before curtain time. She wasn't worried. When she got there she would sing for the people and everyone would be happy.

She was thankful that the Armory was across the street from the train station.

The promoter was worried even though Mahalia's people assured him she would be there.

When eight o'clock came around—but the train hadn't, the promoter panicked and called off the concert.

"She's defaulted, the whole thing's off," he said.

Mahalia's people tried to calm the promoter, but to no avail.

At 8 p.m. the train arrived and Mahalia got off. Mildred explained the situation to Mahalia. By the time they got to the Armory at 8:15 p.m., the promoter had already dismissed the crowd. Mahalia's people had a sneaking suspicion that maybe the promoter didn't have the money to pay Mahalia and was trying to find a way out.

Without a word Mahalia walked to the front door and announced her presence.

"I'm here and I'm ready to sing," she said. "If you find a church somewhere—or if you will bring a piano here on the street, I'll stand here and sing for you for nothing,"

For two hours Mahalia sang at a church that had been opened at her request. She kept her promise. She didn't charge a thing. When the audience insisted on taking up a collection, Mahalia turned it over to the church.

That night back in her room, Mahalia thanked the Lord for not allowing the devil to ruin the event, or her name with the people.

Then there was the time a friend of hers (Prof. Stearns) invited her to visit Music Inn in Lenox, Mass. He wanted her to show musicologists what gospel music was all about.

Mahalia didn't have a problem with that, although she did wonder what the heck a musicologist was and what they did.

Soon after arriving at Music Inn, Mahalia discovered she was not only expected to sing, but also to answer questions.

This would be one of the first times that social science experts would hook up with experts in the art of "Negro folk music."

After settling in, it was time for Mahalia to take the stage. She figured the first thing she would show white people—is how to clap.

"No-no, you got to clap on the off-beat like this, see?"

Mahalia was sincere. She moved on though, leaving the audience to practice on their own.

The Five Blind Boys of Alabama followed in Mahalia Jackson's footprints and became a hit in the 1950s. Thirty years later they were still one of gospel's top groups.

Meanwhile, she began to sing.

The audience was pleased. Some of them clapped. Some on the beat, some off the beat. Oh well, Mahalia had tried. But as long as they got the real message, she was happy.

She was quite uncomfortable with the question and answer period, but she struggled through it while the musicologists struggled with trying to dissect her music.

Her sound and technique was so unorthodox, so different, so untraditional. But the results were tremendous.

Said one musicologist: "Miss Jackson, when you come right down to it, doesn't your gospel owe a lot to jazz?" Mahalia looked at him for a few minutes before answering. "Baby, don't you know the devil stole the beat from the Lord? When you go home, you tell 'em that."

Things were moving fast and furious for Mahalia now.

The blessings began to flow even more. In 1954 she was asked to host her own half hour radio program on a CBS station in Chicago.

Mahalia wanted to perfect a show that would be of interest to the general public, not just blacks.

Joe Bostic wasn't thoroughly convinced that CBS would do the show. He was very concerned that it might be racial. He was skeptical about whether the network would worry too much about the reaction they were certain to get from the people in the South.

CBS wanted an all-black, half-hour, religious show for its Sunday morning lineup. They auditioned Mahalia for the show, and, remarkably it became a television program one year later. Mahalia was ecstatic. She had always wondered whether she would ever be accepted for herself and not treated differently because she was black.

Each week Mahalia, who would have guest choirs on the show, would bring the roof down with her renditions of "Joshua Fit the Battle of Jericho," "Summertime," "Didn't it Rain" and anything else she sang.

Feeling more confident each week about the program's potential, Mahalia asked a question one day that left the Jewish and Irish sponsors speechless.

Why not make the show a national program?

Disappointment filled Mahalia's heart as she was told that no sponsor who sells his product down South would take a chance on a black singer. They would be too afraid that the southerners wouldn't like it. While things seemed to be changing on the outside, the inside was a reminder that racism was still prevalent across the United States.

Mahalia had temporarily lost sight of how powerful racism could be while she was over in Europe. Over there it didn't matter that her skin was a few shades darker than that of white people.

But she was back in America now. She had to wake up and smell the coffee. She was still a black woman and the South was still the South.

Still Mahalia saw hints of progression.

Her second Carnegie Hall appearance was a tremendous success, with both whites and blacks coming out with an enormous show of support.

Mahalia Jackson had become the toast of the town. That was no easy task in a city like New York where audiences were considered traditionally tough.

Even the reigning national columnist and radio personality, Walter Winchell , looked forward to Mahalia's second performance.

He said, "Carnegie Hall will be packed to hear Mahalia Jackson. You never heard of Mahalia Jackson? She's merely the world's greatest gospel canary!"

She received accolades from others as well including, Ed Sullivan who called her "a very fine artist" and Downbeat magazine which called her "the top figure in the field during the last decade."

More than 3700 people lined the streets hoping they would be one of the lucky individuals to get to see Mahalia at Carnegie Hall. Joe Bostic had crammed the arena to its capacity with more than 300 folding chairs placed on the stage and even more throughout the auditorium.

Once again, people had come from as far away as Massachusetts and Connecticut to get a glimpse of gospel's queen.

Even though the opening acts (James Cleveland and the group, The Gospelaires) were good, the audience was still anticipating the shine of Mahalia.

Finally, she walked on stage. A hush fell over the room. You could have heard a pin drop. Mahalia stood still. The lights came up and Mahalia began to sing. "Just as I am, without one plea, but that Thy blood was shed for me."

Tears poured down her face as the spirit began to move throughout Carnegie.

Once again, a racially mixed audience had found a common fondness. Even if they didn't get along any other time—at Mahalia Jackson concerts everyone was as one.

After Carnegie Mahalia's popularity began to magnify by leaps and bounds. She was invited to appear on several television programs.

Throughout her long and busy career, Mahalia Jackson was hospitalized several times. She is shown in Chicago's Little Company of Mary Hospital following a tumor removal.

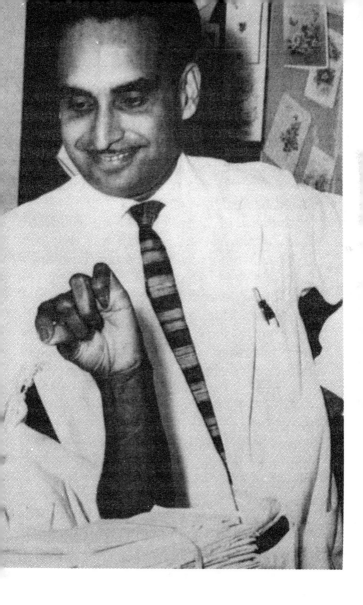

Both blacks and whites wrote fan mail after she appeared on shows like Dinah Shore, Steve Allen and Ed Sullivan.

On her initial Ed Sullivan appearance, Mahalia not only sang her heart out, she also proved she was not a woman who could be pushed around.

Mahalia had been booked on Sullivan's "Toast of the Town." Sullivan was very sensitive to pleasing a wide audience. Ever since his second show, when the singing group The Ink Spots appeared, Sullivan had made a well intentioned effort to have "Negro" representation on the show. After all, this was a time when "Negroes" were starting to speak out against only seeing whites on television. When she arrived at the studio, Mahalia wasn't very impressed. In fact, she was rather happy to discover that both she and the "big folks" rehearsed the same way. While they waited for rehearsal, Mahalia and Mildred Fails decided to check out the piano and organ. To her surprise she was told, even though she had requested one, there was no organ.

Needless to say, Mahalia wasn't having any of it. She promptly insisted that she needed an organ—right then and there. The production crew apologized—but to no avail.

Mahalia filed past them all and asked where

she could find Mr. Sullivan. She was told he was in his dressing room and he couldn't be disturbed.

Before they could finish their sentence, Mahalia had already knocked and invited herself into Sullivan's dressing room before he had a chance to respond.

Sullivan was shocked as he stood there in not much more than his underwear.

Mahalia closed the door so the two could talk in privacy. She reminded her host that she had informed them of her need for an organ prior to her arrival, and once again stressed her disappointment in not having one.

Sullivan reportedly said Mahalia was "mad as hell."

"I really didn't want to give her my only organ," he said. But, of course, he did.

Mahalia sang "Dig A Little Deeper," at Sullivan's request.

"She gave a tremendous performance," he said. "We loved her. She was just so natural; she didn't give a damn whether they [the audience] were black or white or yellow."

The audience liked Mahalia immediately. They didn't care that she was a black woman.

To the network's surprise, the Southern reaction was just as positive as the Northern reaction. Everyone enjoyed Mahalia because she was a great singer. CBS got a load of mail—all of which was a show of support. They loved Mahalia.

Mahalia never wanted to be treated differently just because she was a popular singer. Maybe she was naive to think that things had changed just because she was spending more and more time with whites and getting a larger white following.

On stage white people loved her. But once the show was over Mahalia felt she was being treated as if she had leprosy.

Mahalia Jackson, or no Mahalia Jackson, when it came to getting served in a restaurant in the South—the task was futile. On the road there were no places to eat or sleep. Some gas stations refused service for gas *and* the restrooms. Mahalia and her group would have to turn off the main highway and drive miles out of the way in order to get boarding and gas. Living on fruit during the day and driving half the night in order to make the next concert in time became a regular routine. When it was time for her to sing, Mahalia would be exhausted.

As a Christian and civil rights activist, Mahalia could never understand why white folks hated and feared black folks.

"I don't think the majority of blacks want

to be spending half as much time with the white man as he worries and frets himself about," she said. "All we want are nice homes, places to eat and sleep. We want to be able to buy things at the same stores and the same right to education. We've got our own social and family life that is rich and satisfying."

Mahalia didn't want her statement to be misinterpreted. She was not a racist. She didn't have anything against interracial marriage either, although she was concerned about the black man leaving behind the black woman who had worked and suffered along side him ever since slavery. She wondered who would make the black woman feel important.

"It's been the black woman in the South who has shouldered the burden of strength and dignity of the black family. If a black man wants to marry a woman he can be proud of, there's no need for him to seek out a white woman."

When she was a young woman about 50 percent of black businesses were run by black women. Being pro-black did not necessarily mean Mahalia was anti-white, far from it. She was interested in equality for everyone. It was natural for her to be interested in seeing the black race prosper in education and business.

Chapter Eight

The Church

MAHALIA BELIEVED THAT formality should not be a church requirement.

She always felt that the white church was more strict than the black church. And while she couldn't prove it and had nothing to base it on except her gut feelings, she was convinced that blacks preferred attending their own churches because they could clap their hands, sing the praises and testify in a more comfortable atmosphere.

That kind of activity was not readily seen in the traditional white churches.

To be sure, these hunches were generalities

St. Louis Cathedral in New Orleans. As a child Mahalia could walk from home and admire the church but "only rich people went there. It was the grandest building I knew of then."

since there were several occasions while Mahalia was performing that she would look into the audience and see white people moved to tears just like blacks.

A newspaper man asked her, "Why do the white people really come to hear you sing?" She answered, "Well, maybe they tried drink and they tried psychoanalysis and now they're going to try to rejoice with me a bit. If more white people only dared let themselves go and show their true deep feelings maybe some good might come of it. "

There are all kinds of churches for all kinds of people. Those who like a more spirited service and those who appreciate a more structured meeting place.

Mahalia had seen them all. She had been on the road for more than a decade and had averaged about two hundred concerts a year.

But she didn't want to do concerts her whole life. She did have plans for her future. Those plans included becoming an evangelist (if the Lord saw fit) and building a nondenominational, nonsegregated temple in Chicago to bring talented Christian singers, actors and dancers together, who otherwise would have nowhere to hone their crafts.

Mahalia truly believed that some young black people were cut down due to discrimination. And that the end result was a broken spirit. She tried desperately to turn people around. She cautioned them not to let what had happened lead them to believe that's how things had to be.

When they would ask for her help, Mahalia would tell them, "It takes time to be delivered by the Lord. If the Lord can bring me this far—take me out of the washtubs and off my knees scrubbing other people's floors—then He can do as much and more for others."

The sand in Mahalia's oyster was when people took gospel songs that symbolize the strength of blacks and commercialized it. She despised it when people took the gospel in nightclubs and put out "pop gospel" songs. "They are blaspheming the Holy Ghost," she'd say.

Mahalia never sought to commercialize her own songs. In fact, she had two styles: one for blacks who like an uptempo beat they can tap their feet to, and one for those who like religious songs sung for them.

Deep down Mahalia had a desire to reach the masses through television. The problem was, television never seemed to be the right setting but there were always concerns about time. Mahalia didn't believe in rushing the Lord because of time.

One Easter when she wanted to sing "But Surely He Died on Calvary" on the Dinah Shore show, she was told by Shore, "for you to sing that song the way you'd like would take about five or six minutes and they wouldn't know what to put on after you finished."

Time was not the only concern for Mahalia, it was image. Producers often tried to change her style and look to that of a more commercial entertainer. Mahalia would have none of it. Those things which she could control, she did. But those she couldn't, she grinned and beared it.

For instance, she couldn't get away from the big orchestras that would always crowd the stage when she was performing. Nor could she control being placed between a comic and dancers, who notoriously took up all of the time.

It soon got to the point that Mahalia, although she loved reaching the masses, dreaded the thought of dealing with some directors and producers. She said it was like "going through hell and damnation."

But in the end, all the commotion was worth it because she was sure she'd had a good effect on people. This was evidenced in the many letters she would receive acknowledging that fact. Some wrote they had turned away from alcohol, despair and other manners of negativity as a direct result of her music.

Mahalia was more sure than ever that she had the right assignment.

One of the happiest times Mahalia ever had on television was the time she was invited to sing on the Wide Wide World Christmas program. Mahalia had already planned to go home to New Orleans for Christmas. That was alright with the producers, they could hook it up where Mahalia could sing from her old church in New Orleans.

Mahalia agreed and convinced some of her old friends that she used to sing with, to join her.

She also took a walk down memory lane. She visited all the places she used to frequent as a little girl. She was reminded about the river where she used to sing, the places she lived and the clothes and food she had received from the white people.

Christmas day people poured into the streets and down to the church where Mahalia would perform. The church was packed with people who had known Mahalia when she was a little girl. They were proud of Halie and they had come out to support her.

Mahalia sang "Born in Bethlehem" and "Sweet Little Jesus Boy."

The show was a success. Mahalia was sure that the 10 million who had tuned in to watch were not disappointed.

After the program it was time for Christmas dinner. There were so many friends and relatives that both Aunt Duke's and Aunt Bessie's homes were used as dining areas.

Mahalia received a number of calls and telegrams of praise. She was truly overwhelmed.

The next day after everything had settled down, Mahalia went shopping. Of course, she was recognized on the street. The weather that day was warm and Mahalia began to feel weak. She wanted desperately to sit down in a restaurant and rest a while. But there was no retaurant nearby that would serve a black person.

Mahalia thought how sad it was that she was getting well wishes from white people across the country, but she couldn't get a drink, or a taxi in her hometown of New Orleans.

Unfortunately for Mahalia she realized that New Orleans was not where she belonged. It's a nice place to visit, but she didn't want to live there any longer.

She belonged in Chicago.

Mahalia and Louis Armstrong, the great jazz trumpet player and band leader. Armstrong, two decades older than Jackson, also came from New Orleans.

Chapter Nine

Home Sweet Home

EVERYONE DREAMS OF OWNING their own home and Mahalia was no different. Her long, hard struggle over the years had finally allowed her the financial freedom of buying a home in Chicago.

She was living in a nice apartment, but still there was nothing like your own place, with trees, a garden and a yard.

And besides, she had spent years living in hotel rooms and other people's homes as she wound her way around the world singing the gospel.

She grew tired of being told by tenants to

Mahalia Jackson in the late 1940s, and well on her way to world fame. In this country her recording company, Columbia, had already sold several million copies of her records.

pipe down, even though she enjoyed singing around her house while she cooked and cleaned.

Even after she bought her own apartment building tenants continued to ask her to hold off from singing. She simply had to have her own home where she could scream to the top of her lungs, if she so desired.

So she began to scour the suburbs on the South Side of Chicago. She'd look for neighborhoods she liked and then look for homes that had "For Sale" signs.

While searching for a home Mahalia got a rude awakening. Sure, white people loved to hear her music. They would watch her on television, buy tickets for her concerts and even telephone to say job well done. But they still didn't want her as a neighbor.

During her laborious hunt she was told the homes had already been sold, or that they had changed their minds about selling the property.

Reluctantly Mahalia went to a real estate agent who found a white surgeon who was willing to sell Mahalia his home. He lived in a nice neighborhood and was very familiar with her work.

So were the other neighbors, but that didn't stop them from holding meetings in an effort to find ways to keep the black gospel singer from moving in.

When they realized the doctor was serious about selling his home to a black woman, all hell broke loose.

Mahalia started receiving threatening phone calls at her home at all hours of the night. People warned her that if she moved into the house they would blow it up. They threatened bodily harm as well.

Mahalia had always been a strong woman. But she had to pull double prayer duty on this one. She prayed almost constantly for the Lord to guide her in the way that she should go. She didn't want to start World War III, she just wanted to a nice place to live.

She bought the home.

Soon thereafter her home became target practice. Bullets were shot through the windows so often that police had to be called in to protect Mahalia. They were posted outside her home for nearly a year.

Still, Mahalia was convinced that eventually everything would be all right. She was wrong. One by one the whites moved out and blacks moved in. Whites were convinced that their property values would depreciate and the neighborhood would become a slum.

They were wrong. The neighborhood soon

After gaining world fame, Mahalia Jackson purchased this brick house in the white Chicago neighborhood of Chatham

Village. After moving in, Jackson received threatening telephone calls and gunshots were fired through her windows.

*"I been 'buked and I been scorned," she would later sing.
And some of it came when she was working as a maid, a*

young woman struggling to become a gospel singer, at Chicago's Edgewater Beach Hotel.

I KNOW PRAYER CHANGES THINGS

SING YOUR FAVORITE SONG

WORDS AND MUSIC BY
ROBERT ANDERSON

FEATURED BY
MAHALIA JACKSON
Price 25 Cents

PUBLISHED BY
ROBERT ANDERSON'S
GOOD SHEPHERD MUSIC HOUSE
7824 S. WABASH AVE. CHICAGO, ILL.

EXCLUSIVELY DISTRIBUTED BY
THE ROBERTA MARTIN STUDIO OF MUSIC
1308 E. 47th Street, Chicago 15, Ill.

filled up with doctors, businessmen, lawyers and their families. It was just like any other neighborhood. The people were proud of their community and kept it nice and clean.

Mahalia once joked, "The same birds are still in the trees. I guess it didn't occur to them to leave just because we moved in."

On this sheet music cover the name of the writer was still more important than that of Mahalia Jackson. Although the song was an old standard, Mahalia made it a hit again.

Chapter Ten

Meeting Martin

Not LONG AFTER MAHALIA was settled into her house, she went to sing at the Baptist Convention in Denver, Colorado.

It was there she first met the Reverend Ralph D. Abernathy, who was pastor of the church in Montgomery, Alabama, where the convention was founded.

She also met Martin Luther King, Jr., who was pastoring his first church in downtown Montgomery.

She already knew his parents through their frequent meetings at the various conventions over the years. At that time the elder King was

Dr. Martin Luther King, Jr. Mahalia met Dr. King in the mid 1950s, when he was pastoring his first calling, at Dexter Avenue Church in Montgomery, Alabama. He would start the civil rights movement there.

the pastor of the Ebenezer Baptist Church in Atlanta. His grandfather, the Reverend A. D. Williams, was the force behind the church which had become one of the leading houses of worship for Atlanta's blacks.

A lot of activity was stirring during this time. It was 1955, almost a year after the Supreme Court decided that segregation in the country's school system was unconstitutional. This didn't sit too well with white folks in the South.

An added coal to the fire was the trial that was surrounding Rosa Parks, a black seamstress who started a civil rights movement on her own by refusing to give a white man her seat on a public bus.

Parks was arrested and blacks around the country were outraged. History was made when more than twenty five thousand blacks refused to ride the bus. The protest would last for a year.

MLK Jr. took the lead and organized car pools through the Montgomery Improvement Association. Through the churches they were able to raise enough money to maintain the car pools to get blacks to and from their jobs.

During their initial meeting, Abernathy and King had asked Mahalia to sing at a rally to raise money for their Montgomery Improvement Association.

She agreed. She went to Montgomery and stayed with the Abernathys.

The rally was held at the Methodist Church in Montgomery. Thousands turned out for the rally, which was an enormous success. Whites were more than a little upset and decided to strike back at this blatant move to change history.

Two days after Mahalia left the Abernathy home, it was bombed, as were several of the community's churches and homes of many of the ministers.

Black women were fired from their jobs and black men were told to leave the area.

Still the blacks could not be moved. The boycott against the bus company continued. The protest started to break the bus company which had to resort to charging its white passengers twice the fare.

The next year the Supreme Court decided that segregation on the city's busses was unconstitutional.

Things were starting to change, slowly, but surely. Blacks were more determined than ever to correct a wrong.

Even though whites were clearly resisting the changes with force, MLK Jr., like Mahatma Ghandi before him, was preaching nonviolence.

Mahalia and MLK became good friends. Whenever he came to Chicago, he would stop in to visit Mahalia, who, of course, would prepare a feast.

She was impressed when King and his friends would talk about the movement. She was happy to be a part of it. Her respect for King grew when she realized that his assignment was to lead black people to equality.

Out of the many meetings, the Southern Christian Leadership Conference (SCLC) was born. Whites had their own organizations to thwart the momentum among the blacks. Nothing worked. Blacks persevered.

During that same time Mahalia was honored at a reception in Washington, D.C. She later was invited to sing at Constitution Hall, the same venue Marian Anderson was barred from in 1939 because she was black. This time the place was filled with blacks, who packed the hall to hear Mahalia.

In 1958, she sang at the Newport Jazz Festival. In 1959, she was invited to sing at President Dwight D. Eisenhower's birthday celebration in the White House.

In 1960, the sit-ins began in Greensboro, North Carolina. Blacks began to walk into drug stores, libraries and other public places with the intent of being served. Even when they were being pummeled by whites, the protestors continued to practice nonviolence.

Within two years the sit-ins had spread throughout the South.

The civil rights movement was in full swing. Blacks were fed up and they weren't going to take it anymore.

The country began to sit up and take notice. Even older blacks who had spent many years hiding in the shadows, were getting involved.

It was evident, the country would never be the same.

1960 proved to be a very interesting year. The presidential campaign was in full swing and sit-ins had spread to Georgia.

Martin Luther King Jr. was getting arrested yet another time for his many sit-ins and protests.

Mahalia decided that one of the things she could do was raise bail money for King and his followers whenever they were arrested. And they were arrested often.

"In this world, you got to have a made-up mind," Mahalia once told her friends who had agreed to help her raise the funds. "No straddling the fence."

Of course, Mahalia did not receive any money personally for her efforts. She made it clear to her friends, that, they too, were working *gratis*. She also stressed how hard she wanted them to work on King's behalf.

Down South the protests were beginning to intensify. The protesters were met with fire hoses and police dogs. More than 2,000 people would be arrested. That meant 2,000 bails.

That made Mahalia even more determined. She encouraged everyone she knew to do whatever they could in the form of donating services or wares.

A huge fundraiser was planned and Mahalia got the Mayor's office to donate the 5,000 seat Aerie Crown Theatre in McCormick Place.

Mahalia was hoping to raise about $50,000 for Martin Luther King, Jr. She was determined. The pledges topped $50,000. Mahalia had counted the money personally. She would sleep well that night. Before going to bed she put the money away. She would hand the money over to King in the morning.

When she woke her excitement about having reached her goal continued. Once again, she counted the money. Only this time $5,000 was missing. She couldn't believe it. She counted the money again. What was wrong? She had her suspicions but couldn't prove anything.

When King arrived for the money, Mahalia

handed over $50,000. She had gone to the bank before he arrived. She didn't want a scandal so it was easier for her to replace the money than start a full investigation, which could prove to be embarrassing.

King, who appreciated Mahalia's hard work, continued his non-violent protests.

When King was arrested, President Eisenhower chose not to get involved. Coretta Scott King was worried about her husband. She worried that he could be hurt while in jail. She needed someone to calm her fears.

Presidential candidate John F. Kennedy called King's Coretta and tried to calm her nerves. The next day King was released. Kennedy would prove to be a good friend to the civil rights movement, King and Mahalia.

One day in the midst of the election Mahalia received a surprise phone call from actor Peter Lawford who wanted her to sing at a big Inauguration gala celebration for President Kennedy. Frank Sinatra was producing the party. They wanted Mahalia to sing the "Star Spangled Banner" for them.

When Mahalia got to D.C., she was amazed at the number of celebrities who were involved in the celebration. Everyone from Nat King Cole, Sidney Poitier, Ella Fitzgerald and Harry Belafonte to Milton Berle, Bette Davis and

Jimmy Durante were there.

The party was a success. Later that evening President Kennedy came over to thank Mahalia personally for opening the show.

Mahalia felt proud and emotional the next day as she watched Kennedy take the oath of office. She could feel his strength and felt confident that he would be a good president. She especially applauded his stance on civil rights.

On November 22, 1963, Mahalia Jackson cried like a baby. She always considered herself a strong woman. But when the news came that President Kennedy had been shot and killed in Dallas, it was more than she could bear.

Her emotions were running rampant—so much so, that she collapsed. She couldn't believe it.

"So young, so much promise."

Kennedy had become a friend. Now he was gone.

A television station, KNXT, invited Mahalia to come to the studio and sing a song in honor of the fallen president.

As she stood before the microphone, Mahalia's eyes began to swell. The memories came rushing back.

She sang "Nearer My God to Thee." It would be years before she would ever sing the song again.

Civil Rights protesters in Alabama in the early 1960s. They, both black and white followers of Dr. King, were beaten, jailed and some, again white and black, were murdered.

Chapter Eleven

On The Road Again

ONCE AGAIN, IT WAS time for Mahalia to go on the road. She and her accompanist Mildred Falls jumped into the Cadillac, and off they went on a tour that would take them from New York to Texas.

Many nights were spent on the road between concerts. The one-night stands were beginning to take their toll. A lot of her strength was being drained. But Mahalia pressed on—determined not to disappoint her fans, or herself.

She thought of home often and missed the intimate times she would have with close

---

President John F. Kennedy proved to be a good friend to Dr. King, Jackson and the civil rights movement. She sang "The Star Spangled Banner" at the Inauguration celebration for Kennedy.

friends.

After two months of one-night stands, she got the call to do another European tour. Of course Mahalia agreed, but only after it was agreed she could see the Holy Land this time around.

She was booked to tour six countries—saving the Holy Land for last. Right after her last concert in Texas, Mahalia, Mildred and a young reporter who would handle to press on the tour, drove to Chicago and then caught the train to Washington D.C. where a bon voyage party was being held in her honor.

The Under-Secretary of State Chester Bowles hosted the reception at his home. He and his wife were big fans of Mahalia's. The reception was a success. Mahalia felt honored and humbled by the experience.

After another reception given to her by friends at a church in Washington, it was off to New York to board the *United States*, which was set to sail for Europe.

Almost as soon as the ship pulled away from the dock, Mahalia began to feel ill. Her rigorous schedule had taken all her energy.

It was like *deja vu*. Eight years earlier, during her first European tour, it ended with her being flown home to a Chicago hospital.

Mahalia couldn't believe this was happening

again. Unable to venture out on deck, she lay in her bed for two days, too weak to leave her room. She worried that she wouldn't be able to sing once she got to Europe.

Finally, she saw a doctor who informed her that her blood pressure was low. He put her on a special diet and within days she started feeling better.

This was Mahalia's first time on an ocean liner. She loved the water. She would sit for hours in her cabin and listen to the waves.

When her strength returned she decided to attend a party that was being given for comedian Jackie Gleason. An hour later she was back in her stateroom looking out the window at the water, which she found to have an enormous drawing power on her.

During the Easter Sunday morning service, she sang "Were You There When They Crucified My Lord?" As she sang the boat began to rock. Both she and Mildred began to feel seasick. But they rode out the waves and continued singing.

When the ship docked Mahalia felt like royalty. Waiting for her was a welcoming committee and a long, black stretch limousine that would take her all the way to London.

When she arrived in Europe, reporters asked her how she liked being a second class citizen. The statement made Mahalia mad. "If I would tell you, and you've never been one [a second-class citizen], you wouldn't know what I was talking about."

She wasn't about to bad-mouth her country. "I don't know any place that I love better than the United States," she said. "With all its shortcomings, it's still my home."

First on the agenda was a taping for a television program. Mahalia enjoyed the experience. The musicians learned her music quickly, the choir sounded almost as good as the choirs in the states and everybody was friendly.

The big event came the next night when she was to perform at Albert Hall. The last time she was there was a bad experience. She was so sick it was the first time she really didn't think the audience had received her best. That first time in 1952 Mahalia weighed only 140 pounds. This time she was a hefty 240 pounds. Still, one of the head men at the hall said she looked well.

The morning of the concert, once again, Mahalia felt weak. She prayed and ate a lot of spinach and liver. Soon she was feeling better.

She took a walk outside of the hall to get some air and to clear her head. She had worried about this concert ever since she left New

York. The first time, the audience was a bit cold. She was determined this time to leave her mark on their hearts.

After practicing a while with Mildred, Mahalia felt better. Her strength had returned and she began to swell with excitement.

The hall was sold-out. It was standing room only. Mahalia was overwhelmed. She felt as if the Lord was giving her another chance.

She began the concert with "My Home Over There." It was one of her favorites because it reminded her of the Apostle Paul when he said, "I've fought a good fight and kept my faith."

Mahalia was a success. The audience cheered, stomped their feet and clapped their hands. She didn't know who was in the audience, but she was sure they had felt her music. She described them as a "religious revival audience."

Mahalia had truly arrived. When the concert was over, she was mobbed as she tried to leave through the stage door. In fact, she was knocked to the ground and had to crawl to the car on her hands and knees.

When she got to her hotel room, Mahalia couldn't believe how exhausted she was. Not too exhausted to get on her knees and thank the Lord for blessing her with a successful concert.

Mahalia was sure the rest of the tour would be a success as well.

Now it was on to Frankfurt, Germany where she performed at the Kongresshalle. The surroundings were not the best. It seemed everything that could go wrong, did. The dressing room was cold and had very little furniture. The stage didn't seem as if it could hold Mahalia's weight. The lights were inadequate and the microphones left much to be desired.

Mahalia and her agent David Haber let the manager of the concert hall know just how unhappy they were with the conditions. The manager was rude, but Mahalia didn't care. If he would not improve the conditions, she would cancel the concert.

After giving the manager an earful, the concert went on and the German audience seemed to love every minute of it. So much so that they wouldn't let her go home. She did about twelve encores before going to her dressing room to change, only to come back out and sing some more. The concert went on so long the police were called to remove the audience from the theater.

The next day the *Daily Express'* headline read "Thousands There But Mahalia Sang To Me."

On to Hamburg where Mahalia went shopping for crystal for her home in Chicago. She wanted to be able to serve her guests in grand style. She bought everything from cake dishes, to goblets and coffee mugs.

That night when she sang at the Hamburg Musikhalle, it was another triumph for the woman who was acting as the "unofficial Ambassador of Good Will" in England, France, Germany and Italy.

Everything was perfect, the piano, the acoustics, the audience and especially Mahalia.

Again the audience was so enthusiastic—they literally forced Mahalia to change her clothes and continue the concert in a plain street dress and Indian moccasins.

After using ground transportation to get to each concert, Haber convinced Mahalia to take a plane instead so that she wouldn't be so tired.

After a horrible train ride to Berlin, Mahalia agreed.

In Berlin she performed at the Sportspalast, which, because of its size, can be compared to New York's Madison Square Garden. Again the audience was zealous. The manager of the hall told Mahalia he hadn't heard such cheers since 1938 when Hitler delivered a speech on that very stage.

That comment left Mahalia a little uneasy. Hitler had preached hatred. She was there to sing the Lord's word. The reviews were marvelous. One man said she was a miracle. Another said she was the greatest thing that ever happened to Hamburg.

Denmark was next. Mahalia had made it through the airplane ride. Admittedly, she was a little nervous during the flight, refusing to move until the plane landed.

Thank goodness it was not as tiring as a rickety train ride. In Denmark the concert was good, but the house was not full. Still, Mahalia was getting a warm feeling from the audience. One man said he and twenty-four of his friends had come just to hear Mahalia sing "Silent Night." She obliged and cried when she finished. Denmark was a success and it was on to Paris.

When they landed there was no hoopla because the whole country was under martial law because of the Algerian revolution. It was still up in the air whether or not the concert would go on as scheduled. In the meantime, Mahalia and Mildred went shopping.

They rode down the Champs-Elysees, drove past the Church of the Sacred Heart and went to see the Cathedral of Notre-Dame, the Eiffel Tower and the Louvre Museum.

Like Germany, the audio equipment at the Olympia Theater in Paris was poor. The piano wasn't in good condition, the dressing room was small and the auditorium was rundown. Again Mahalia had to give someone a piece of her mind. This time it was the concert manager who had booked her European tour.

The concert was victorious for Mahalia. The French had given her a wonderful welcome. She was even welcomed by jazz greats Melton (Mezz) Mezzrow, jazz critic and club organizer Hughes Panassie and Duke Ellington's arranger—pianist Billy Strayhorn. After the show, there was such a big crowd of people waiting outside the stage door that Mahalia and her entourage couldn't leave.

She went back to Germany to sing in Munich and Essen. On the train ride through Germany Mahalia thought: "I sat and looked out the window and saw all those green fields and the lovely houses, all set so close together just like the people really love each other."

While the concert halls in Germany were still cold and drab, Mahalia was content that the audiences were warm and loving. She received numerous encores. She sang so long that the microphones were finally taken from the stage as a means of getting the crowd to leave. Mahalia kept on singing and Mildred kept on playing. They wanted to hear "The Lord's Prayer" before she left.

She obliged.

Rome was another stop on her tour. Mahalia agreed with the custom of closing down for three hours each day after lunch.

She thought St. Peter's Basilica was magnificent. While there she met Pope John, who gave her his blessing. He sat upon his throne and gave a sermon. Because they had special invitations she was able to go into the private quarters of the Pope.

Even in the Vatican Mahalia had to duck autograph seekers as she tried to escape into a small side room on the way to the Pope's quarters. To get to his quarters they had to climb a long flight of stairs, then up an elevator before being led into a room with a marble floor that looked like a mirror. Mahalia and her party had to wait about thirty minutes before they were called into a smaller room with a fabulous ceiling and a Papal throne. They lined up before being ushered into yet another room where they waited a little longer before being ushered into another room. Finally, the Pope walked in dressed in white.

Later that afternoon, Mahalia, Mildred and Al went to lunch at Posetta's where they met actress Susan Strasberg and singer-dancer

Josephine Premice.

From Rome it was finally time to board a train for Naples to catch a ship called the *Esperia*, which would sail them to the Middle East.

For as long as she could remember, Mahalia had wanted to visit the Holy Land. She was finally on her way.

When she got to the Egyptian port of Alexandria, Mahalia was met with culture shock.

There was lots of noise, heat, different smells and lots of meat hanging outside with bugs flying around. For a woman who was meticulous about a clean kitchen, it was a little much to take.

When they arrived in Lebanon there was lots of traffic and confusion. The drivers in New York were wonderful compared to the drivers in the Middle East.

On the day that she would finally visit Jerusalem, Mahalia got up early to prepare for the trip. She already had a sense of being in another land at another time. She could just imagine how she would feel once she made it to the Holy Land.

On the way there she had to endure a roller coaster ride through the winding, dusty and narrow road. Mahalia and her driver were like oil and water. He would speed, Mahalia would complain. This went on for hours. While racing through the desert Mahalia continued to holler at the driver, who insisted he had never been treated that way before by any woman. He quickly decided he wanted to visit the United States and marry Mahalia.

Mahalia jokingly told him he had "missed his chance" and that she would never marry a man who drove the way he did.

The first stop was the River Jordan. Mahalia walked slowly down the bank. She knelt down to let the water flow through her hands. She couldn't believe how muddy the water was. From there it was on to the Dead Sea and then the hills of Jericho.

The Holy Land left Mahalia speechless. She was overjoyed with having the chance to see the places she had read about in the Bible and sung about in songs. And now here she was walking the same streets where Jesus had walked and praying at Calvary.

The next day she drove through the hills of Galilee and on to Bethlehem. The road was crowded with donkeys, oxen and people traveling on foot. Mahalia was in awe as the guides led her to a big arched hall, which is where one of the world's oldest Christian churches stood on the site of the inn where Mary and Joseph had sought lodging. Taking time out to pray, Mahalia was once again overwhelmed as she saw the spot where the manger in which Christ was born stood.

The guide escorted Mahalia to the cobblestoned streets of Old Jerusalem, which was filled with people, music and shouting. Once again she was speechless as she walked the same path as Jesus had when he bore the cross. Being there drained everything out of her. She cried when she came up on the spot of the Crucifixion.

This experience would always have a special place in Mahalia's heart. She had seen the place where Jesus was born, touched the Rock of Calvary. Her dreams had been fulfilled.

To top it all off, she had a wonderful concert in a Tel Aviv concert hall in Israel.

Because Jerusalem was divided into Arab and Israeli sections, Mahalia and her party had to get out of the cab they were riding in on the Arab side and unload their bags which were carried across the boundary line by a porter. Then they had to walk about 50 yards across the no-man's land.

Mahalia was tired. The three-month European tour was beginning to wear a little thin. Whenever she was through singing, Mahalia would go back to her room and think about home. There's no place like home.

Chapter Twelve

Glory Hallelujah!

DURING THE LAST TWO decades of her career, Mahalia had become a national institution.

She sang in concert halls, theaters, jazz festivals and several times at the White House, which included the 1961 presidential inauguration. She also sang for important gatherings of Martin Luther King's Civil Rights Movement, and even before crowned heads in Europe.

She had become a Hollywood celebrity by appearing in several movies, including "St. Louis Blues" (1958), "Imitation of Life"

Jackson, often in poor health but a tireless worker, especially for political and civil rights causes, is again in the hospital in 1964. Here with her husband, Sigmund Galloway.

(1959), and "The Best Man" (1964).

She had won numerous awards including, the Charles Cors Academic Award in 1950 for the best folk records and a year later, Le Grand Prix Du Disque. Greater Salem Baptist Church cited her outstanding achievement in giving and making the spiritual blessing of song. WLIB in Harlem gave her its "First Annual Voice of Liberty Award" for being "A World Symbol of Dignity." The National Academy of Recording Arts and Sciences awarded her two certificates for the "Best Gospel" of other religious recordings, "Great Songs of Love and Faith." Then there was the citation for "Promoting the First Religious service on TV, (and) for being the first religious CBS TV and Radio Star."

On the 100th Anniversary of the Emancipation Proclamation, she received a Merit Award plaque from the Committee of the American Negro Emancipation Centennial. There was also the medal for the Grand Army of the Republic, in commemoration of the 100th anniversary of the birthday of Abraham Lincoln. She also received an "Award of Distinction" from the Civil War Centennial Commission .

There were other awards as well. But the glitz and glamour never impressed Mahalia. Her agenda never changed. Her assignment was to work for the Lord through song, and to work for herself through being active in the civil rights movement.

When she returned from the Holy Land she found a lot of discontent and chaos. This was about the same time that the Committee for Racial Equality, who called themselves Freedom Riders, were challenging the archaic practices of the South. They no longer wanted segregation in public places. Their desires were not greeted favorably by the whites, who wanted to keep the blacks in their place.

Mahalia was concerned about all the violence that the Freedom Riders were being met with as they ventured deeper into the South.

Although she was already widely known for her music, Mahalia's fame increased during the civil rights movement. She was one of a number of black and white celebrities who attached themselves to the movement, developing close personal relationships with the key players, Martin Luther King and Whitney Young Jr. Mahalia knew changes would not come easy. Some people would get hurt, others would die.

In May 1961, some of the Freedom Riders boarded a bus for the South. Ten days later the bus with the first group was bombed and burned by segregationists outside Anniston, Alabama. The group was also attacked in Birmingham and Montgomery. Finally, Attorney General Robert F. Kennedy had to dispatch four hundred U.S. marshals to Montgomery to keep order in the Freedom Rider controversy.

Nevertheless, the violence continued.

Mahalia kept a close watch on the movements of the Riders and on Martin Luther King Jr., whom she had befriended. She often held rallies to raise bail money for King and his followers who would often get arrested after demonstrations.

She thought highly of King and denounced those who tried to make it seem that King and his followers were divided.

A soldier in the fight for equality for all mankind, Mahalia was especially disappointed in those prominent blacks in the church who refused to take a stand in the civil rights movement. She wondered why instead of pitching in to help they were trying to bring the movement down by not supporting King and Abernathy's heroic and humanitarian efforts.

She was happy, however, that a large percentage of the fight for freedom down South was coming from the church and from the gospel songs people were singing. She believed that

the "Freedom Songs," like "We Shall Overcome," had become popular because they
spoke a language to a person's soul that
couldn't always be expressed in words.

"There's something about music that is so
penetrating that your soul gets the message."
Against the wishes of some members of the
National Baptist Convention, Mahalia held a
rally for King. It was the first time she had
actually gone against the wishes of the Baptist Church. Initially, she had tried to find
some preachers in Chicago to present King,
but none had stepped forward. She couldn't
believe it. But there was not time for too much
disappointment, there was a lot of work to do.
She didn't have time for people who couldn't
quite make up their minds on which way to go.

"In this world, you got to have a made-up
mind," she said. "No straddling the fence."

So Mahalia hosted King's visit to Chicago.
She ordered limousines and organized the
press—stopping at the *Chicago Defender,*
Johnson Publications and even dropped in on
Mayor Richard Daley, who would do anything
for Mahalia. Celebrities turned out for the ral-
ly, including Aretha Franklin, Dick Gregory,
Shelly Berman, Dinah Washington, Eartha
Kitt and Gloria Lynn, plus local choirs.

Nearly 100,000 people turned out for the

rally at Aerie Crown Theater in McCormick Place, which raised $50,000.

Mahalia couldn't physically get too involved with the movement. Her health was not at its peak. Her manager, Lew Mindling, even had her checked into a hospital for tests.

The doctors found her heart was strained because of the many years on the road.

Headstrong and determined, Mahalia left the Little Company of Mary Hospital room one night and proudly announced to the nurses that she was going home to continue her recuperation. She would spend the rest of the summer resting. That is, until that lovely summer day in August.

The March on Washington in 1963 was an important and impressive gathering that saw blue and white collar workers, politicians, celebrities and the like converge on the Lincoln Memorial for a common cause. The gathering was for jobs and freedom.

It was a peaceful gathering that sunny day in August. More than 250,000 persons (60,000 whites) had come from every corner of the U.S. and overseas, by any means necessary, to take part in a ceremony that would prove to be one of the most important events in U.S. history. The March on Washington demonstration was, at that time, the largest civil rights demonstration ever.

Blacks and whites prayed together in the shade of the marble figure of Abraham Lincoln which glistened in the morning sun. Gathering on the grassy slopes of the Washington Monument, they walked a mile to the Lincoln Monument where they repeatedly voiced their disdain with having to wait more than 100 years and 240 days for freedom. They waited patiently for the numerous dignitaries to gather on the speakers' platform for what was hoped would be some words of wisdom and commitments to change.

For three hours they listened as speaker after speaker demanded passage of a civil rights bill and the implementation of the Declaration of Independence, and the Thirteenth, Fourteenth and Fifteenth Amendments.

Something this important could not be missed by Mahalia. For years she had been an advocate for the rights of everyone, but especially blacks. She sang benefit concerts whenever she could in order to raise money for the civil rights movement.

That afternoon she gave her own words of encouragement by singing the spiritual, "I've Been Buked and I've Been Scorned." You could have heard a pin drop amongst the thousands who had crowded the platform. The song's message burned a sad recollection of the injustice that blacks had to endure in America—into the hearts and minds of those in attendance. The moment was emotional and had an enormous impact on the crowd, many of whom had begun to sing, clap and cry.

Mahalia, who had sung the song at the request of Dr. Martin Luther King Jr., was also emotional as she let out a gutteral "Glory Hallelujah!". She felt the words she sang—because she too had lived with a great deal of racism and discrimination.

She remembered the time she and her husband were refused service in a downtown Chicago restaurant. There was also the time she was making a picture for Columbia in California and the producers, two white men, invited her and her accompanist out to lunch at a plush restaurant. When Mahalia and Mildred arrived suddenly there were no tables available.

Mahalia's sense of humor and her strong faith, helped her escape the battles with prejudice and ignorance.

When she recalled the March, Mahalia would say "It was the first time in my life that I saw my race of people united together, and it was something my very soul enjoyed." Mahalia knew the March on Washington was "the work of the Lord."

It was on this day that King gave his memorable and moving "I Have A Dream" speech. "I have a dream that one day this nation will rise up and live out the true meaning of its creed," he began.

Mahalia, who had often given her wages to the civil rights movement, was moved by King's speech. She admired him for his unselfish efforts.

She had just as much respect for President Kennedy, who, Mahalia felt had done more than any other American president to bring equal rights to blacks.

She was in California on November 22, 1963. She was leaving her hotel to do a television show when she heard the bad news. President Kennedy had been shot and killed. Mahalia prayed it was a mistake. "Oh, no. Jesus!" she cried.

Memories of Kennedy came rushing back. She thought back to the first time she noticed him at the Chicago Convention in 1952. She felt he had an untimely death because "he wanted to bring about our freedom." She wondered how many others would have to die before the country came around.

Chapter Thirteen

I Do,
Again

MAHALIA TOOK THE DEATH of President Kennedy very hard. She tried to shake it, but the thoughts of his efforts and the senselessness of his death, played havoc with her mind.

She found solace and comfort in the arms of a handsome man named Sigmund Galloway. Galloway was tall, soft-spoken and cared for Mahalia very much.

Although he lived in California and she in Chicago, they got together whenever Mahalia went to Tinseltown to record some songs or perform in concert.

Mahalia Jackson not long before she passed on "to a higher place than this" as she often sang. Her funeral in New Orleans was attended by thousands of fans, friends, and family.

Mahalia considered Galloway just a friend, although those around her saw something more romantic brewing. Mahalia continued to deny it was more than a platonic relationship.

Her marriage to her first husband, Ike Hockenhull, had ended when she was only 30 years old. Because of her incredible schedule, she hadn't had time to concentrate on romance.

Jokingly, or maybe not so jokingly, Mahalia frequently said to her concert audiences, "Out of all the good-looking men I see here tonight I ought to be able to find myself a husband!"

She insists it was all a harmless joke. No one believed that except Mahalia. Sure, she had made the church and her career her whole life, but she was still a woman.

Mahalia knew Galloway's family very well. They were good church people. Galloway, who was in the building business, was a widower with a little girl named Sigma. He also had a musical background having played in an orchestra and even been an arranger.

Galloway first met Mahalia at a Columbia Studio lot in California when a friend of his who was playing for her recording session invited him to go along.

Mahalia sang "Take God by the Hand." Galloway loved her singing.

"I though to myself, a woman who can sing like that must be very warm inside. When she finished, I walked up and introduced myself."

They began to see more and more of each other. Their friendship became much tighter and Mahalia, who by this time was calling him "Minters," began to look at him in a different way. He became her regular escort to dinner parties and other Hollywood functions.

The romance was cut short when Mahalia went back to Europe for some more concert dates. When the tour was over she could think of nothing but home and Galloway.

Mahalia got tired of coming home to an empty house and an empty heart. The loneliness was so loud, she was ready to share her life once more.

On the way home from Europe she fantasized about what it would be like to be married again.

Two months later, in 1964, Mahalia and Minters were married. It was no surprise to her manager Lew Mindling, who had predicted it even before Mahalia knew she was attracted to Galloway. It was an intimate ceremony. Mahalia was still tired from the tour. She wore her best blue dress and a corsage of white orchids as she and Galloway exchanged vows in her living room.

Mahalia was determined to make her house a happy home.

After the wedding Mahalia and Sigmund went downtown to the Top of the Rock restaurant to watch the lights of the city. Mahalia Jackson Galloway was happy.

Unfortunately, the marriage wouldn't last. In 1969 Mahalia and Sigmund divorced.

When asked how she felt about being divorced twice when her life is so close to the church, Mahalia replied, "It's because I feel that I was meant to give my life to the church that it had to be that way, and I'm not ashamed of it."

Ella Fitzgerald, long an admirer and friend to Mahalia Jackson, was just one of the many celebrities that attended her funeral.

Chapter Fourteen

Goodbye!

A FTER MONTHS OF DECLINING health, the voice of Mahalia Jackson was silenced on January 27, 1972. The woman whose soulful gospel renditions thrilled fans all over the world, had fought a long and hard battle, but lost.

She died at Little Company of Mary Hospital in a south Chicago suburb after checking in January 19 suffering from an intestinal condition. Hospital personnel said the last two days of her life, Mahalia was in a semiconscious state. She died without any of her friends or admirers at her bedside. The im-

Mahalia Jackson at a fundraiser. Once she became famous, she constantly allowed her name to be used to promote charitable causes she believed in and if possible would show up herself.

mediate cause of her death was heart disease. She was 60 years young.

That was not Mahalia's first trip to the hospital. Over the years she had been hospitalized on several occasions dating back to 1964. The reasons were primarily exhaustion from her demanding itinerary. She cut her European tour short during an appearance in Germany in 1971 suffering from a heart ailment.

For years Mahalia, considered a national treasure, had suffered from a heart condition. Still, she refused to stop touring, instead opting to cut back on her grueling concert schedule. In previous years she had made few public appearances because of health reasons.

The woman who first won fame as a gospel singer in the choir at Greater Salem Baptist Church on Chicago's south side in the 1940s, had built a career that spanned 45 years.

Her best known recordings included, "He's Got the Whole World in His Hands," "Precious Lord," "Move On Up A Little Higher, " "Just Over the Hill," "How I Got Over" and "I Can Put My Trust I Jesus."

One of the great success stories in gospel music, more than 6,000 Chicagoans came out to pay their respects to the woman who had rightfully earned the title, "world's greatest gospel singer."

Not even the terribly cold January weather could keep away the 50,000 people who had silently filed past Mahalia's mahogany bed the day before the funeral.

As Mahalia would have wanted, her funeral was not a time for sorrow, but rather a celebration of her life. The thousands who attended the funeral remembered the way Mahalia's life had touched others in such a positive way.

Every day of her life commemorated the life of Jesus. She never gave herself recognition, but rather reminded people that she was just an instrument of the Lord. She truly loved the church and was adamant about giving God the glory. At a young age she had promised to "dedicate my life to Him in song".

Mahalia believed she was ordained to sing the gospel and that her singing was a ransom of gratitude for God delivering her from the many trials she came upon during her life.

The two-hour funeral, held at the Aerie Crown Theater was attended by celebrities, politicians, dignitaries, family, friends and fans, which included Sammy Davis Jr, Ella Fitzgerald, Mayor Richard J. Daley, Aretha Franklin and Coretta Scott King, who eulogized the singer as "a friend—proud, black and beautiful."

Remarkably, the same events happened three days later at the Rivergate Convention Center in New Orleans where the rich, the poor, school children, whites and blacks paid their respects.

Mahalia laid in state with an honor guard drawn from U.S. and city services, in what was probably the largest, most elaborate final rites given a private citizen at that time.

Those in attendance included Lou Rawls, Louisiana Gov. John J. McKeithen, Mayor Moon Landrieu and Dick Gregory.

Gregory said of Jackson, "she was a true moral force in the world; soldiers draw soldiers; entertainers draw entertainers, and politicians draw politicians. But a moral force draws all people and that's why so many people all over the world were attracted to Mahalia Jackson."

It seemed everyone who had known and loved Mahalia wanted to say goodbye to the woman who had brought so much joy to so many people.

Although there was an enormous outpouring of respect and affection for Mahalia, she had once said she wanted "no big fanfare when I'm gone."

Mahalia, who received a star on the Hollywood Walk of Fame in 1988, didn't exactly get her wish, as more than 24 limousines drove past her childhood church, Mt. Moriah Baptist Church, where she was baptized 48 years earlier. Singer Aretha Franklin, one of Mahalia's favorite artists closed the rites in Chicago by singing "Precious Lord, Take My Hand" and singer Lou Rawls sang "Just A Walk With Thee."

Still, the funeral procession was without a marching band and their was a quiet interment at Providence Memorial Park in Metairie, Louisiana. One by one they came to praise her.

Mahalia was a special woman with a special gift. Her success was even more gratifying because of her humble beginnings. Because of her childhood, Mahalia had a dream to build an interdenominational temple with its own religious school.

She revered education. She was especially pleased when she was invested with the hood that made her an honorary Doctor of Music during a ceremony at Marymount College in New York in May 1971.

Her temple had been a dream she had for years because she wanted to give all children a religous education. She wanted her temple to be a place where anyone could come and worship, as well as learn.

She had saved more than a quarter of a

million dollars for the project, which, she said, would teach people not to be bitter because "when you are bitter, you spread it around you." Of course music would play a dominate role at the temple. Through song Mahalia hoped to lift people's minds above poverty, sickness and discrimination.

Her hope was that whatever was wrong in the world, through song and faith, tomorrow would be better.

Minters Galloway said of Mahalia, "She was a highly talented singer, one who'll be hard to replace." Neither Galloway, nor Hockenhull were in Mahalia's will.

Galloway died of cancer four months after Mahalia's death. Hockenhull died within the year, and successively, Mildred Falls and Aunt Hannah Robinson.

Some people said of Mahalia, "you could just see God in her eyes and feel His spirit in her singing."

Mahalia knew that her time on earth was growing to a close, but she never worried about death.

"A believer in the Lord doesn't worry about dying."

INDEX